I WAS THERE

by

JR Snook

Published by Caboodle Books Ltd 2020.

A Catalogue record for this book is available from the British Library.
ISBN: 978-1-9997749-7-4
Page Layout by Highlight Type Bureau Ltd, Leeds
Printed and bound by Short Run Press Limited

The paper and board used in this book are natural recyclable products made from wood grown in sustainable forests.
The manufacturing processes conform to the environmental regulations of the country of origin.

Caboodle Books Ltd.
Riversdale, 8 Rivock Avenue,
Steeton, BD20 6SA, UK.

This book is dedicated to Mum and Dad....

Thank you for my sporting genes!

Bernard

Maybe not quite as tense
as that famous penalty
shoot-out - enjoy!
best wishes
Jn Smith

Author's Note:

I have been waiting for the right moment to write this book, which I started planning over ten years ago. The subject of the book is LIVE Sport, specifically relating those sporting events that I attended in person. From the many events witnessed, I have narrowed down the list to what I consider to be the most impactful and memorable, which I hope will jog memories and make for an entertaining and informative read.

Sport has always played a big part in my life, and there is nothing quite like playing sport. The thrill of competing either as an individual or as a team member is hard to beat. Thousands of us have felt the emotional highs and lows as sportsmen and women, but very few of us have the luck or the talent required to play sport at the highest level. Yet, we all have our own experiences to draw on, and this is perhaps why we all have an opinion on the game we are watching.

Television and more recently the plethora of pay to view platforms have brought great sporting genius and drama into our living rooms like never before, but this does not deter the die-hard fans amongst us from attending sporting events in person, and experiencing first-hand the sometimes drab but often thrilling aspects of live sport. Admittedly it can be an expensive business these days to buy tickets to watch Premier League football matches, or a day of Test match cricket, or a day at the Open Championship. It can also be a bit of a lottery to try and obtain tickets for global events like Wimbledon or the Olympics.

On the other hand, and perhaps this is a generational thing, it can also be too easy to always watch from the comfort of your own home. Yes, there are plenty of amazing live sporting moments I have watched on TV, and there are particular times of the year which I always look forward to, for example in early April when we are often treated to a "super" weekend of sport, which might include FA Cup semi-finals, The US Masters and the Aintree Grand National all in the space of 48 hours. We cannot be in two places at once, and we are therefore indebted to the advances of technology which allow us to be transported to multiple sporting venues around the globe on satellite and terrestrial television from the comfort of one's own favourite armchair, by the mere touch of a button.

However, being there in person, and witnessing live sport has its own essence. It provides a different level of involvement and authenticity, and with others around you, be they family, friends or strangers, there is a shared experience and atmosphere which you cannot get in your living room. The crowd, be it in the hundreds or the thousands, on any given day creates its own unique atmosphere, and I suppose that is the added unknown of watching live sport.

I was lucky to be brought up into a sport loving family at a time when it was more affordable to buy tickets for matches, but my advice today would be to make the best of both worlds. On the one hand, take advantage of the increasingly bespoke and competitively priced offers that enable you to be more specific about the nature of live sport you want to stream into your home, whilst on the other hand, put some money aside every year, choose the events you really want to see, and remember different venues have unique atmospheres, book your tickets well in advance, and preferably plan to go with family or friends as well.

Going to watch live sport does not guarantee value for money, or wall to wall excitement, and there are definitely days, usually cold days on the football terraces, when an afternoon in front of the fire would have been preferable. But we are drawn back again and again by the unpredictable nature of live sport, a mere spectator to swings of momentum and fortune, extreme weather perhaps, a crucial dropped catch, a forward pass, a lucky bounce, a poor refereeing decision, an incredible piece of individual skill, and more currently an intervention by camera technology...any one of these can impact on proceedings.

Great sporting moments generally just happen when they happen. I consider myself very privileged to have been able to witness so many, and by the same token, disappointed to have missed even more. I am not a professional sportsman, nor a commentator of note, but I do have a unique collection of sporting memories with accompanying insights, anecdotes and statistics to share with you.

I hope you will enjoy this sometimes nostalgic and personal journey gathered together over the last five decades, and which covers a range of different sports including Football, Cricket, Golf, Horse Racing, Motor Racing and the Olympics. Played out at some of our favourite and most recognisable sporting venues, I have also tried to describe the context of the sporting moment, the gamut of player and spectator emotions, from unbridled joy to disbelieving tragedy, as well as uncover some of the background stories relating to our sporting heroes who play such a major part in each individual chapter.

As a footnote, there is a strange irony to the timing of this book, because coronavirus has changed the world we live in to the point that professional sport is being played in empty stadia. To enhance viewer experience, broadcasters are even offering the option of artificial crowd noise and some sports have now been allowed to let a small number of socially distanced supporters back into grounds, whilst players, management and media exist in their own 'bubbles'. This must all seem very strange for the players, so let us hope we get back to normality soon, when our sporting heroes can once again perform and entertain in front of capacity crowds.

Foreword
By John Helm

It is somewhat ironic that I have been able to make my living as a broadcaster in radio and television as I am a great advocate of watching sport in the flesh rather than from the armchair.

Obviously I do watch quite a lot of sport on the box – but believe me if I have a choice of a Premier League match in my own home or going out on a freezing cold day to take in an Evo-Stik thriller or a game of rugby league, I plump for the latter.

There's nothing like being able to say "I was there".

Over the past 60 years as a working journalist I have been monumentally fortunate. I have been to ten football World Cups, four Olympic Games, four Commonwealth Games, 20 Open Golf Championships, and umpteen other sporting jamborees that people would pay a fortune to attend.

I've seen Maradona and Messi, Nicklaus, Palmer and Woods, Sobers and Stokes, Usain Bolt achieving peaks of professional performance that mere mortals witness in total awe.

We all have our personal memories of feats that enthralled and astonished us at the same time. Anyone who has played sport at any sort of level can appreciate the magnificence of the best – who are true artists.

Even when covering a sport which in all truth I knew little about it was easy to see why certain people were in a different class to the rest – Torvill and Dean, Franz Klammer and Steve Redgrave spring to mind.

You didn't need to be an expert in ice dance, downhill skiing or rowing to recognise true genius when you saw it.

Robin Snook has clearly embraced the beauty of watching sport at close quarters from an early age. I suspect like me he knew he was never going to be good enough to win Olympic gold or a Claret jug, so opted for the best alternative.

Funnily enough when he talks about the 1976 Open golf championship at Royal Birkdale and a player known the world over by just one name – Seve – I have a different memory of the same event.

Defending champion Tom Watson shot an horrendous 80 – yet was still gracious enough to grant me an interview for BBC Radio – proof to me that sport is not just about winners and losers but also about the way in which people conduct themselves through the peaks and troughs of performance.

This is another beauty of being an attendee. You get the whole picture of the event. The atmosphere, the buzz and the thrill that never leaves you on recounting personal memories for many years to come.

"I Was There" is a personal crusade of a true sports lover and all the better for it.

Acknowledgements

As I have discovered, writing a book is both a rewarding as well as a daunting undertaking. I am therefore indebted to a great many people who have supported and encouraged me, as well as provided their own recollections of the same events I have described.

In particular, I would like to thank my wife Emma, who I think has been grateful that I had a project to keep me busy during lockdown, and to my son James with whom I have enjoyed a number of the adventures described in this book, and to my daughter Joanna who contributed significantly to the cover design. In addition, I would like to thank my parents for my sporting genes, which have allowed me and my siblings to play and enjoy sport.

As each chapter in the book relates to a particular time and event, I have thanked individuals in the section at the end of this book entitled Bibliography, additional sources and thanks. I would also like to thank those people who have provided professional guidance. Firstly Tony Hannan, for pointing me in the right direction; John Helm for agreeing to provide a foreword; Angela Lawless for her patience and skill in setting, formatting and proof reading; Trevor Wilson for allowing me to publish under the Caboodle Books imprint, and Joseph Witchall for the final cover designs.

Contents

Chapter   Page

1. The Magic of the FA Cup – February 1976 13

2. Centurion of Centurions – August 1977 23

3. The Boy from Pedrena – July 1979 41

4. The Miracle of Headingley – August 1981 62

5. Only a 4 to win the Open! – July 1983 79

6. Escape to Victory – March 1985 100

7. Phoenix from the Ashes – May 1985 109

8. I Saw Adelaide Alive – November 1985 123

9. Beware Bowlers Who Bat! – December 1985 . .151

10. A Day at the Races – July 2005 161

11. The Greatest Match Ever Drawn? –
    August 2005 169

12. Doctor Needed! – December 2006 186

13. I wish I was an Olympian – August 2012 200

14. Taking Root – July 2013 210

15. The Home of Golf – July 2015 220

List of Images

Page

1.   Bolton v Newcastle programme cover 129

2.   Boycott batting at Headingley 130

3.   Seve Ballesteros at Royal Lytham 131

4.   Headingley 1981 - letter from the BBC
     acknowledging my poem "Testing Time" 132

5.   Tom Watson, chipping at Royal Birkdale;
     staff badge from 1983 .133

6.   Bradford City Team 1984-1985 134

7.   Bradford City Fire Disaster Programme 135

8.   Bradford City Memorial picture by Paul Town   .136

9.   Adelaide Alive Poster 137

10. Royal Ascot York 138

11. Parade Ring, Royal Ascot, York 139

12. Kevin Pietersen's Ashes shirt from 2005 140

13. WACA, Perth 2006 141

14. London 2012 stadium 142

15. Lords – Ashes scorecard, 2013 143

16. St Andrews 2015 144

Chapter 1:
The Magic of the FA Cup

Saturday 14th February 1976 – Burnden Park, FA Cup 5th Round

There were very few sports that I had not had a go at by the time I got the chance to watch my first FA Cup match in February 1976. Every daylight hour away from the classroom was spent outdoors kicking a football, or striking a cricket, golf, hockey or tennis ball, and running, cross-country on Ilkley Moor, or athletics in the summer. Indoors, there was also table tennis, snooker, chess and trampolining to enjoy.

However, and inspired by the 1970 World Cup Final with Pele, Jairzinho and Carlos Alberto, football emerged as my first sporting obsession. This was also the time of Brian Clough's Derby County who won the 1971-72 First Division Championship from three teams, Liverpool, Manchester City and my favourite team, Leeds United. Can you believe it, just one single point separated all 4 sides, with Arsenal, Tottenham and Chelsea a few points further adrift.

Many of my friends were Leeds fans, and it didn't take me

long to follow suit, and I remember receiving my Leeds shirt as a birthday present, and quickly black felt-tipping on the number 7 in homage to my favourite player, Peter "Hotshot" Lorimer. I started writing a diary in 1973, and the entry for May 5th simply reads: "watched FA Cup Final, Leeds lost. Pity." This loss to Sunderland and Jim Montgomery's outstanding save from my aforementioned hero had not put me off supporting Leeds, not at this stage at least.

My first live football match followed 2 years later when I was taken to Elland Road and I saw Leeds United come from behind and beat West Ham United 2-1 on Saturday 11th January 1975. I also got a Leeds scarf, and I was also allowed to stay up and watch Match of the Day, still to my mind, the best television highlights programme around.

I also remember very clearly a comment made in the Leeds crowd that day when West Ham had the cheek to take the lead, through a powerful downward header by their Bermudian born striker, Clyde Best. Behind me, loud and clear, one Leeds supporter shouted out "Get back on your bloody reservation, Best." It meant absolutely nothing to me at the time, but how sad that 45 years later, racism still haunts the game at both club and international levels.

Many commentators call football the beautiful game, and back in the 1970s I was young enough and innocent enough to believe this to be true, and looking back through rose tinted spectacles, I don't disagree with my younger self. The 1974 World Cup only helped to demonstrate the point further, when the final matched Holland against West Germany. West Germany were strong and well marshalled by captain and legend Franz Beckenbauer, Holland, their football as bright at their orange shirts, were led by possibly the most gifted of European footballers of all time, Johan Cruyff.

All my school mates wanted to be one of the Dutch, whether it was Jan Jongbloed in goal, midfielder Johan Neeskens or Johan Cruyff himself, or in my case striker Johnny Rep. Like in so many stories, the fairy tale ending was not to be, with Gerd Muller cancelling out a penalty each, turning on a sixpence and winning the trophy 2-1 for the Germans. And history was to repeat itself four years later when in a classic final Argentina defeated Holland 3-1. Holland who had given the world total football were denied the ultimate crown, losing two consecutive finals, each to the host nation, and ever since they have flattered to deceive but for one spectacular European title.

The FA Cup was all part of the beautiful game too. It was an English institution. You just never knew when the next big cup shock was going to happen. How good would it have been to witness first hand Ronnie Radford's pile-driver out of the Hereford mud against mighty Newcastle United?

Cup shocks even happened in Cup Finals too – as evidenced by Sunderland in 1973 and Southampton in 1976. The decade of the seventies saw no less than nine different winners, all a far cry from today's big money, big team superiority, where a cup shock is more of a collectors item. Admittedly, they do still happen, and few will forget Bradford City's stunning 4-2 victory at Stamford Bridge when the lowly visitors overcame a 2-0 deficit at Jose

Mourinho's all conquering Chelsea in January 2015.

Before the 2008 Cup Final which saw the unfashionable Portsmouth and Cardiff vie for the coveted trophy, the previous 12 finals had been won by the big four, Liverpool, Arsenal, Chelsea and Manchester United. This is the price of the success of the Premier League which sadly now sees the FA Cup as a second class competition, with some ties now decided on the day, without a replay.

So to restore our collective faith, I want to take you back to February 1976, to a time when the FA Cup was the biggest domestic football prize of all. I recall great anticipation at school, when the headmaster announced that one of the boys parents was providing 12 tickets to see an FA Cup 5th round tie.

To ensure fair play was seen to be done, a draw to see who would be the lucky recipients of these tickets would be made a week before the match which was to take place on Saturday 14th February at historic Burnden Park, the then home of Bolton Wanderers. Ours was a small school of 50 boys, so the odds of getting a ticket were high. To this day I don't know whether being captain of the 1st X1 football team improved my chances of getting on the bus, but sure enough I was included and off we went to Bolton to see what turned out to be a cracker.

By now my love affair with Leeds United was on the wane. This no doubt had something to do with Leeds' decline in fortunes, and another cup shock, this time at the hands of lowly Colchester United. Perhaps it had more to do with my father's persistence in asking me to go to Valley Parade to watch Bradford City.

This process had started in the late sixties when Bradford boasted two league clubs. Then, Bradford Park Avenue was my father's club of choice, but not mine. As the story goes, considerable pressure was being placed upon me to watch a game at Park Avenue, something that I was desperate to avoid for reasons unknown. After lunch, and to avoid being dragged to the game, I got on my bike and disappeared for 5 hours. My eventual return home coincided with the arrival of the local police who had been looking for me, my mother's wrath, and my father's return from the match where he had witnessed an unprecedented 7-0 home victory for the soon to be relegated Bradford Park Avenue.

Now more of a Bradford City fan, but still with strong feelings for Leeds United, I remember arriving at Burnden Park that winters day full of awe at the size of the ground, the sheer volume of people, both in terms of the noise levels as well as the numbers (46,880 people attended) and the electric atmosphere that both sets of supporters created, which for a party of 12 and 13 year olds was completely new, as well as being quite intimidating. I remember wondering which side to support. I had no allegiance to Bolton Wanderers or their visitors that day, Newcastle United. On the rare occasions when you are impartial at sporting contests, it is easier to appreciate the game for what it is, even to applaud good play by either team.

Both teams contained some big names, and at the time of

the match Wanderers were riding high at the top of Division 2, whilst Newcastle United were mid-table in Division 1. Wanderers had home advantage, and a shock was definitely on the cards, but I remember siding with Newcastle for some reason, perhaps because I liked their kit colours more, perhaps also because being a budding goal scorer myself, this was a chance to see the prolific Malcolm Macdonald in the flesh.

Bolton Wanderers now have their home at the out of town once named Reebok, now University of Bolton, stadium. Back in 1976 though, Burnden Park was as I recall, an old stadium then with huge high wooden stands at the sides, open terraces at the ends and what appeared to be a raised playing surface surrounded by a narrow walkway allowing only minimum space for a corner taker to run up.

Burnden Park looked a grey football fortress. A packed crowd was there to see the game, and what a noise they made. From our position just about on halfway, we looked down from one of the covered stands and had a great view of proceedings. When Sam Allardyce headed in after five minutes for the home team Burnden Park erupted, and if you don't believe me, just look the highlights up on YouTube!

Malcolm Macdonald was in no mood to disappoint me or his many other fans, and his first goal came in the 32nd minute, following a long ball over the top by Tommy Cassidy. Supermac latched onto it, a clever first touch with his head, and a deft touch with the famous left foot to take keeper and defender out, saw the ball calmly passed into the now unguarded goal. This was the finish of an expert striker, who was at the peak of his game, who had that uncanny knack of knowing exactly where the goal was at all times.

And just before the half-time whistle, the magic moment happened. Newcastle were pressing in the Bolton half, and won a throw in on the left touch line. To put this into context, I was sat close to half way and was exactly in line with the thrower, and had the perfect view of what happened next, and I have never forgotten the simple brilliance of it.

The throw was quickly taken by left winger Tommy Craig and I could see Macdonald drift towards him, pulling a defender with him, and he quite clearly gestured with his right hand to his teammate to throw the ball to him so it would come across his body, and then all in a moment, he swivelled on his better left foot and on turning towards the Bolton goal, as the ball dropped after its first bounce, he unleashed an unstoppable 25 yard volley from just outside the left edge of the box with his less heralded right foot into the top right hand corner of the net, only losing his balance after the perfect strike had been made.

All this happened in my direct line of sight, and I don't remember seeing a greater live individual goal. The Newcastle fans went crazy, the Bolton faithful were stunned to silence, and Barry Davies' commentary says it all… "What A Goal". This set up beautifully for an end to end second half, which saw Bolton fight back to equalize through Garry Jones, only for Alan Gowling to put

Newcastle back into the lead with another superbly taken goal, but Bolton were not done, and defender Paul Jones rose highest to head home the equalizer six minutes from time to round off a breathtaking 3-3 final score line.

I don't particularly remember too much about the match, and that is mainly because it was a very long time ago. However, the one thing that has always stuck with me, and which I can still clearly picture, is the stunning simplicity and quality of strike by Supermac. I reckon I had the best seat in the house to see the whole thing from start to finish, and that's the luck of the draw I suppose, to be in the right place at the right time. It was definitely something we tried to re-enact back at school at football practice, with differing degrees of success.

As was traditional, the match was replayed just 4 days later back at St James Park, in front of 52,760 fans, and despite another exciting contest, there were no goals. In those days there was no penalty shoot-out either, so both teams and 43,448 fans met again for the conclusive third time on the 23rd February, and this time the match was played at a neutral ground, Elland Road, with Newcastle's Alan Gowling scoring the winner in another closely fought 2-1 victory.

Newcastle United failed to make it past the sixth round of the cup that year, losing 4-2 to Derby County at the Baseball ground, despite two more goals from Gowling. For the record Derby's scorers were all household names of the era, Henry Newton, Bruce Rioch (2) and Charlie George. And all the while in the other side of the draw, 4th Division

Bradford City were on a rare cup run, and beat 1st Division Norwich City, before losing in the last eight to eventual winners Southampton, 1-0 at Valley Parade, after a flamboyant Jimmy McCalliog volleyed free-kick from Peter Osgood's scoop pass.

Lawrie McMenemy's Southampton were the underdogs against Manchester United in the final at Wembley, but a goal from the diminutive Bobby Stokes seven minutes from time won it for the Saints.

Those were the days when the FA Cup was the FA Cup – and if it took you three matches to get through one round, and you had to play these matches in the space of just 10 days, as well as your league matches, so be it. (Newcastle also had a trip to Anfield on February 21st). Watching the YouTube highlights with sound just goes to illustrate what the cup meant to the top players and to the spectators, and for good measure the cost of your match day programme would set you back just 10p! (See page 129).

As for Malcolm Macdonald, not only did he give this schoolboy a great sporting memory, he also played 14 times for England, scoring six International goals, of which five came in a 5-0 victory at Wembley against Cyprus in 1975. He scored 95 goals in 187 appearances for Newcastle United, including a hat-trick on his home debut against Liverpool, and it was in this game that he earned the nickname "Supermac" which came from a chant by the Newcastle fans to the tune from the musical Jesus Christ Superstar, being "Supermac, superstar, how many goals have you scored so far".

As a postscript, and many years after the event, I was sitting in a printer's waiting room waiting to pass a job on press, and someone had put a video on to while away the time, and to my great surprise and enjoyment, and under the title of "100 Best Goals", there, and out of the blue, was Malcolm Macdonald's outstanding strike from 1976, almost exactly as I might have imagined it from the depths of a childhood memory.

Supermac is now 70, and retains an avid interest in football through his punditry, and his beloved Newcastle United continues to be a beacon for their fanatical, faithful and long suffering supporters. For the record the 1975-1976 season ended without glory for both Newcastle, who finished 15th in Division 1, and also for Bolton Wanderers who just missed out on promotion by one point, finishing 4th. However, both clubs benefitted financially from their classic cup contest, and incredible to think that over 143,000 football fans attended one, two or all three of the matches needed to decide this 5th round tie. In those heady pre-premiership days, the FA Cup really was magic.

Chapter 2
Centurion of Centurions

Headingley, Leeds: Thursday 11ᵗʰ August 1977

Having played a wide range of sports over the years, including cricket, golf, hockey, football, fives, bowls, athletics, table tennis, squash and badminton, I am often asked which was my favourite sport, and my stock answer is that I have enjoyed all these sports, but team sports have always been the most enjoyable. A friend of my father's once gave me some very good advice when he said that I should play team sport for as long as I could, as there would always be plenty of time later in life to enjoy individual sports like golf.

The one main team sport missing from this list is what I would describe as the ultimate team sport, rugby. It's a game I am sure I would have enjoyed playing, but it was always football at school. When I say rugby, of course I enjoy watching both codes, perhaps because of my Northern roots, which lean towards League, but also because of the annual Six Nations, which arouses such passion amongst the players and supporters of each nation. A quick mention for my grandfather, Dr Bob Hanson, on whose knee I sat during the 1966 World Cup final, but who was an avid supporter of Scottish rugby, and when they played in the Six Nations, woe betide anyone who interrupted the game or Bill McLaren's legendary commentary.

Having been born in Yorkshire, it will come as no surprise to say that cricket was and still is my favourite sport. Consequently watching cricket at Headingley has always been in the blood, and typically I would go and watch the Thursday and Saturday of the Test with my father, traditionally day one and day three. More recently, and with the advent of shorter formats of the game, I have also enjoyed the thrills and spills of T20 cricket with my own family.

However, given the choice, and being a traditionalist at heart, give me Test match cricket any day. My earliest memory of a live cricket match was as a seven year old, and an England v Rest of the World Test match, and with the help of ESPN cricinfo, I can confirm the match took place at Headingley between 30th July and 4th August 1970. The sun shone gloriously and Garry Sobers, yes the great Sir Garfield Sobers, was playing, someone who my father and mother had met in the 1960s when he had spoken at a Northern Cricket Society event.

The series took place only because the scheduled South African tour had to be cancelled for political reasons, reasons which were totally beyond me then, but I was later to understand were all to do with the then South African government's apartheid policy, the situation having earlier been aggravated by England's selection of a Cape coloured player in their team, in what became known as "the Basil D'Oliveira affair".

One interesting element of being in the ground and seeing live international sport, which perhaps only springs to mind when you are writing a book of this nature, is that you can share and compare the names of yesterday's legendary players with family and friends and pass this down generation to generation. Just like my father did to me, when he explained that his father had taken him to Trent Bridge in the 1930s, to see the likes of Harold Larwood and Bill Voce ripping through county championship top orders, as well as International Test stars like Wally Hammond, Hedley Verity and Len Hutton, and Australians like Don Bradman, Stan McCabe and Bill O'Reilly.

And on this occasion, I had the privilege to witness some of those great players who would later be recognised as cricketing legends. For England, there was a recall for Yorkshire's very own opening batsman Geoff Boycott, and two other Yorkshire players were also included in the team, left arm spinner Don Wilson, who would soon become cricket coach at my school, and making his England debut, right-arm fast bowler and left hand-bat, Chris Old. England were captained by another Yorkshireman, Ray Illingworth, and also in the team were Brian Luckhurst, Colin Cowdrey, Keith Fletcher, Basil D'Oliveira, Tony Greig, Alan Knott and Jon Snow. Quite a line up, and it needed to be given the quality of the opposition.

Garry Sobers captained the Rest of the World, and I

particularly remember two South African bowlers, the hostile Mike Procter, and the bespectacled Eddie Barlow, who took all 10 wickets between them in England's first innings of 222, Barlow taking 7/64 with Keith Fletcher top scoring with 89. The Rest of the World replied with 376/9 declared which included 95 by Deryck Murray, and 114 from Garry Sobers.

Also playing for the Rest of the World were Rohan Kanhai, Mushtaq Mohammad, Clive Lloyd, Graeme Pollock, Intikhab Alam, and Barry Richards. England fared better in their second innings also scoring 376, thanks to 64 from Boycott, 92 from Luckhurst, 63 from Fletcher and 54 from Illingworth, thereby setting a modest target of 223 to win. At the end of the 4th day, Rest of the World had been reduced to 75/5, but the following morning Sobers (59) and Intikhab (54) steadied the ship, and despite four wickets for Snow, and four for Illingworth, Richards and Procter saw the Rest of the World home by just two wickets.

In this day and age with the international cricket calendar so crammed full with Test, 50 over and T20 cricket, sad to say it would be extremely unlikely to see the Rest of the World Test X1 being revived.

Despite England, India and South Africa having their short periods of success, there have been two dominant powers in world cricket in the modern era, by which I mean from 1975 onwards.

It took a very special person of character to unify the Island Nations of the West Indies, and that man was Clive Lloyd.

Not only was Lloyd a great captain, he was also an outstanding close fielder, and very dependable and often explosive middle order batsman. He was also well known in England as he regularly played for Lancashire County Cricket Club, and under his leadership the West Indies conquered all before them and for nigh on 20 years, they were invincible, combining Caribbean batting flair with a quartet of interchangeable fast and hostile bowlers, who regularly blew away all comers.

Australia next emerged as the other super power, but only after having survived the difficult early 1980s, when the supremely determined Allan Border took on the captaincy and gradually transformed his nation's fortunes, thanks in part to his nugget like uncompromising attitude, but in the main because of some outstanding emerging talent, which included the Waugh brothers, Ricky Ponting, fast bowling supremo Glenn McGrath and world class leg-spinner Shane Warne, which led to continued success at both Test and 50 over cricket.

The summer of 1976 should trigger good memories for most of us that can remember that far back. Gardeners may recall hosepipe bans, golfers may recall the near burnt fairways at Royal Birkdale where a young Spaniard first made his mark, and cricketers will recall very hard wickets and parched outfields. You may also remember that the West Indies were our visitors that year, and you may recall our captain, Tony Greig, who had made his Test debut in the Rest of the World series in 1970, inexplicably saying England were going to make The West Indies "grovel".

The first Test match of the series was played at Trent Bridge and although the match was drawn, there was early evidence as to who would dominate the series. Friday 4th June 1976 so nearly makes my second entry because I saw, live at Trent Bridge, Viv Richards score 232 of the most sublime yet destructive runs. As a 13 year old, my simple diary description says "Ace Innings", which did not do Richards justice, but it certainly was, compiled against one of England's better bowling attacks of Snow, Hendrick, Old, Underwood and Greig.

Sir Isaac Vivian Richards went on to hit a blistering 291 in the final rubber of the series at the Oval with that memorably scorched outfield, and those trade mark flicks across the line, and those lazy ambled singles, all the while chewing gum in that nonchalant almost arrogant way. I loved watching him bat, and in his pomp there was none better, and he went onto amass 829 runs in the series at 118.42, despite missing the Lords Test due to glandular fever. He alone certainly made England grovel that year!

The summer of 1977 brought the Australians to our shores again. Ashes cricket always has an extra edge and I had enjoyed a taster of it two years previously when Dad took me to the first day of the Lords Test in 1975. Coincidentally, this was Graham Gooch's second Test match, and having been dismissed for a pair in the previous Test at Edgbaston, and with Lillee and Thomson in their prime, another failure here at Lords led to him not being selected again until 1978. However Gooch would go on to be England's most prolific batsman, amassing 8,900 Test runs, a total which was recently surpassed by his own Essex protege, Alistair Cook.

England's most prolific opening batsman in this era was Yorkshire's Geoff Boycott. Boycott was born into a South Yorkshire mining community and quickly found that he had a talent for cricket, joining Ackworth Cricket Club at the age of 10 years old, and winning a Len Hutton batting award whilst he was at Primary School, and at one time playing football for Leeds United U 18's alongside Billy Bremner. However it was Boycott's cricket that got him noticed, playing for the Yorkshire Federation Under 18 team, and also for Barnsley Cricket Club, where he became team mates with two other famous Yorkshiremen, Dickie Bird, and Michael Parkinson. And according to Dickie Bird, it was his application, concentration and absolute belief in himself, allied to his mental strength, that made him stand out.

Boycott made his debut for Yorkshire in 1962, and went on to make his England debut in 1964 as a 24 year old, and he would quickly establish himself as a prolific opening batsman, a role which his personality was well suited to. A controversial figure throughout his playing and non-playing career, no one has ever doubted his brilliance with the bat, and allied to his extraordinary powers of concentration, he was often a thorn in the side of any opposition bowler. His record of 108 Test caps, 8,114 Test runs, at an average of 47.72 including 22 centuries, are clear evidence of his talent and capabilities at the top level. The timeless nature of Test match cricket certainly suited Boycott's method and approach perfectly.

After a long tour of the West Indies, and a single Test against India in June 1974, Boycott made the surprise announcement that he was going into self-imposed exile, citing that he had lost his appetite for Test cricket. Another factor which was well documented at the time was Boycott's differences of opinion with the then Test skipper, Mike Denness, and the more cynical commentators of the day went further and said that Boycott was a selfish man, and was looking after his Test average at a time when Australia's Dennis Lillee and Jeff Thomson, and West Indies pace duo of Andy Roberts and Michael Holding were at their quickest.

Whatever the reasons for his exile, there was in the intervening three years of exile a growing clamour from different quarters for Boycott to return to the England fold for the 1977 Ashes series, and with a new captain at the helm, Mike Brearley, and after the drawn first Test at Lords, and then a convincing victory in the 2nd Old Trafford Test, Boycott was recalled in place of Dennis Amiss for the 3rd Test at Trent Bridge.

England batted first and after two quick wickets, Boycott was joined by local favourite Derek Randall, and the two of them were beginning to forge a good partnership, only for Boycott to push back at a delivery from Jeff Thomson and inexplicably call for a suicidal single. Boycott had a reputation for being a poor caller and runner between the wickets, and Randall had a reputation for backing up too far, and too energetically, but on this occasion the misjudgement of the run was entirely of Boycott's doing.

Picture the image of Boycott standing at the non-strikers end, head in hands, bat discarded and at his feet as if in defeat, realizing his error, as poor Derek Randall had to trudge back to the dressing room, whilst the Australian team converged around him in gleeful surprise at the gift of the wicket. Sometimes it can feel very lonely out in the middle for a batsman, and it takes a certain kind of individual to overcome such disappointment and guilt, and to regroup, and to refocus. Yet through adversity Geoff Boycott had the type of character that could quickly compartmentalise a mistake, put it to one side, and strive to make amends, and bat as long as he could, and to his credit that is exactly what he did, scoring 109, whilst at the other end, another of England's tough characters Alan Knott, would play one of his best innings for England, making 135, putting on 215 with Boycott to lay the foundations of victory.

Boycott scored 80 not out in the second innings as England cruised to a seven wicket victory to go 2-0 up in the series, and returning to the side, he had recorded his 98th first class hundred to boot. Ian Botham made his Test debut in this game, which remarkably saw Boycott bat on all 5 days of the match, which was the first time this had been done by an English cricketer. Clearly Boycott's batting had had a big psychological affect on the opposition, and in a post match interview Botham commented: "The Aussies, shell-shocked at having to bowl at Boycott for 22 and a half hours, capitulated without much of a fight."

And four days prior to the 4th Test, which would take place at Boycott's beloved Headingley, he was at it again, this time in the county championship, scoring his 99th first class century, 104 against Warwickshire at another Test ground, Edgbaston. The stage was set for a very big moment, and all of Yorkshire, and no doubt all cricket fans across the world were suddenly acutely aware where his next game was, and were even wondering whether Boycott had purposefully engineered this situation!

All the pre-match hype and the newspaper column inches were full of Boycott's big chance, and how fitting it would be to reach a ton of tons at Headingley, and I for one, with tickets for day one, was really looking forward to seeing it happen, and hoping against hope that the weather would be good, and England would win the toss and bat. But this wasn't quite the way Geoff Boycott saw things...

In the book "Fire and Ashes: How Yorkshire's Finest Took On the Australians", Boycott recounted the build-up to the game as follows:

"I kept the Post Office busy. A stack of good luck letters, telegrams and cards began to arrive immediately. On the eve of the Test I was still trying to read, let alone reply, to all of them. During our team meeting that evening, Mike Brearley noticed I wasn't my usual self. When I asked to be excused from the general conversation, he didn't hesitate before saying yes, and he didn't need to ask why I wanted to retreat to my room".

Boycott admitted he took sleeping pills to try and get some rest, and woke later than normal the next day, and had to rush to the ground, feeling tired and listless, and at this point he was hoping that his skipper would lose the toss, and England would field. Fortunately for everyone, including me, and all England supporters, Mike Brearley did win the toss, and he and Geoff Boycott strode out to the middle to great cheers. They took guard just before 11am on Thursday 11th August, ready to do battle, Brearley presumably with his own thoughts and aspirations to play a captain's innings, Boycott weighed down with all the pressures of the moment.

Australia made the perfect start, as Brearley was on his way back to the pavilion after just three balls, and England had lost a wicket without scoring a run. After a hesitant start, Boycott began to find his touch, finding the middle of the bat, and in his words "Soon I was middling the ball, and the tiredness began to drain away from me. It was replaced with a solid conviction about two things: this innings had to be treated like any other – and it had to be constructed around the basic principles I'd always employed. Play one delivery at a time; play at the tempo I felt was right for me, and play with a single-minded determination that blocked out extraneous thoughts".

Boycott was dropped on 22 by Rodney Marsh and reached 36 not out at lunch, and continued to bat patiently all day on an excellent day for batting, his trademark concentration and defensive technique never faltering. The anticipation felt by the crowd at the start of the day was replaced by an air of calm once Boycott had seen off the pace attack of Thomson, Walker and Pascoe. (Lillee was not playing in this match). And then I vaguely recall a sumptuous trademark cover drive off Max Walker which brought up Boycott's 50.

Boycott was 79 not out at tea, and the break at least gave

the crowd the opportunity to relax for a moment, but just 20 minutes later he was back out in the middle, sleeves rolled up as they had been all day, wearing his blue England cap, holding his lightweight, by todays standards at least, distinctive County bat, marking out his guard again, adopting that familiar and comfortable stance, in readiness for the next ball.

The Aussies had regrouped too, and thought they had their man, but Boycott survived a huge shout for caught behind off spinner Ray Bright, umpire Bill Alley remaining unmoved to the great relief and huge cheers from the Yorkshire faithful. Next man in, Graham Roope, thought he was out and was already donning his gloves, but had to sit down again, but he was back on his feet soon enough when Tony Greig was clean bowled by Jeff Thomson and as we went into the last hour of play for the day, it was then that the tension levels began to rise noticeably.

Boycott and Roope batted very sensibly together, but the tension grew by the ball, the crowd one minute quiet and anxious, the next minute alive again when the scoreboard ticked on. How Boycott kept the crowd waiting, especially in those nervous nineties, and then he got to 96, and one more boundary would do the trick, or would he do it in singles, or would he fall at the final hurdle?

Boycott was in no hurry, and had no intention of changing his game plan, even when Australia reverted to the part time bowling of Greg Chappell, but sometime approaching 5.50pm the inevitable slightly over-pitched half-volley was gloriously dispatched through mid-on for four, Roope at the non-strikers end having to jump in the air to avoid the ball, and suddenly Boycott's arms were aloft, and there was pandemonium, prolonged applause and pitch invasions.

To a man the crowd stood and clapped for what seemed ages. On the pitch Australian captain Greg Chappell was one of the first to congratulate Boycott, as a posse of well natured supporters ran onto the pitch and surrounded him. What drama, what a setting, what a fairy-tale story, what a release of expectation, what a richly deserved ovation, the perfect place for a Yorkshireman to score his century of centuries!

Geoff Boycott continued well into the second day too, and England, having resumed on 252/4, reached 436 all out, with Boycott last man out in the 156th over for a 191 after 629 minutes at the crease. For the second match in a row he had batted Australia out of the game, and once again he had proved that he was still the best opening batsman of his time.

Australia were skittled out for 103 in their first innings, with young Somerset all-rounder Ian Botham making his mark by taking 5/21. Following on, Australia were dismissed for 248 in their second innings, Mike Hendrick starring with 8/95. England had cruised to another Test victory by an innings and 85 runs, and having taken an unassailable 3-0 lead in the series, had also won the Ashes.

It is perhaps interesting to note that my diary simply states that Boycott scored his hundredth century. His appeal to a young student of the game like myself suggests that his defensive style was clearly not in the same league as Viv Richards's more flamboyant approach. However, with the passage of time, and armed with the knowledge of 40 years of playing the game, and also 20 years of coaching others, it is now much easier to appreciate Geoff Boycott's method and his technique. Casting my mind back to 1977, there was Boycott standing on the balcony of the old pavilion at Headingley at the end of play with a glass of celebratory champagne, surrounded by a large and happy crowd, and surely this was his finest hour.

Boycott may have been 37 years old, but his cricketing career still had plenty more chapters to it, and he was to play a less important role in the 1981 Headingley Test, better known for Ian Botham's daring deeds, but more of that later in this book. He continued to play for England up to 1982, but controversy was never far away, and when he was overlooked for the captaincy for the Indian tour of 1981/82 things turned sour. On this tour he overtook Garry Sobers' career Test run record, but during the tour he had claimed that he was too ill to field in one Test, but this back fired when it was later found out he had been playing golf instead. There were also issues regarding his slow rate of scoring, so he was then dropped from the team.

Later in 1982, Boycott was instrumental in organising a rebel tour to apartheid South Africa, and against the wishes of the Test and County Cricket Board, he and 12 other former England cricketers, who were mostly at the end of their International careers, and led by Graham Gooch, toured in an unofficial capacity, and played Tests and three ODI's. (Also in the squad were Amiss, Emburey, Hendrick,

Humpage, Knott, Larkins, Lever, Old, Sidebottom, Taylor, Underwood, Willey and Woolmer). Despite widespread criticism around the world, the tour was well received in South Africa, but all of the players then received a three year ban, which in effect ended Boycott's international career.

Boycott's career at Yorkshire as a player ran from 1962 to 1986, and he captained the side from 1971 to 1978, and the statistics will show that this period was one of Yorkshire's most disappointing. Boycott was sacked as club captain at the end of the 1978 season, but the infighting between the different factions in Yorkshire had already started, with Boycott often commanding popular support from the wider membership, but not from his playing peers, past or present.

Boycott continued to play for Yorkshire but the bad blood would not go away, and once the Committee had decided not to renew his playing contract at the end of the 1983 season, the Members 84 Group lobbied hard for his reinstatement. The Committee were forced to go back on their words, which led to the resignation of stalwarts like Fred Trueman and Ronnie Burnet, and also Boycott's own election to the full committee, which meant he had a duel role to fulfil now, and of course this could only head in one direction. At the end of the 1986 season, and in the knowledge that Phil Carrick would be become Yorkshire's new captain, Geoff Boycott called it a day, and retired.

Despite all the off-field shenanigans which undoubtedly damaged every party involved, but particularly Yorkshire Cricket Club, perhaps we should look at Geoffrey Boycott's cricketing career purely from a cricketing point of view, and it is worth noting that at the time of his retirement, he had scored more first class runs than any other active player. If 1971 was Boycott's halcyon year, in which he scored four Test centuries and 11 County championship centuries, then 1977 was a pretty good year too with seven centuries in all, so the question of whether Boycott could have engineered his Headingley triumph is an interesting one to ponder on.

He started the summer of 1977 on 93 first class centuries, and so by the law of averages taken over his long career, Boycott would expect to score six or seven tons a season. That being said, no batsman however consistent can avoid a good ball, a bit of bad luck, or a poor umpiring decision, and of course form is temporary. However, when a batsman gets into good nick, he knows, and he tries to stay in this rarified zone for as long as possible, and proverbially make hay while the sun shines.

Boycott's 94th century came at Harrogate against Somerset on June 19th, and this was followed by three back to back centuries in early July. Firstly, Boycott scored 103 at Scarborough v the Australians on July 4th, then he scored 117 at Lords v Middlesex on July 7th, and thirdly he made 154 at Trent Bridge against Nottinghamshire on July 12th. However, surely it was only his recall to the Test team for the 3rd Test at Trent Bridge, and that painstaking comeback 109 on the 29th July which suddenly concentrated Boycott's mind to the possibility of what could happen, but he still needed to score his 99th century to make it a possibility.

So whilst the opportunity of scoring your 100th century on your home ground is something to hope for, Boycott's quest remained just an aspiration, that was until his 104 at Edgbaston v Warwickshire on August 6th. Everything changed after this 99th century had been written into the record books, and those intervening four or five days must have been quite a nervous time for Boycott, as the expectation gathered momentum. It is worth reminding ourselves that the next game was no ordinary County Championship game, rather it was an Ashes Test, and it was at Headingley. Most of us would have buckled under the weight of expectation, but not Boycott, who used his experience, self-belief and mental strength to pull it off.

Since his retirement from the game, Geoff Boycott has carved out a successful career on the airwaves, passing on his great knowledge to cricket listeners with his no nonsense style of commentary which has at times been controversial. Unafraid to ruffle player egos, he has also coined a few memorable phrases which include "corridor of uncertainty" and notably of dropped catches that "his mother or grandmother could have caught that in her pinny", or, of an easy batting miss, that they could have hit it "with a stick of rhubarb". Boycott announced his retirement from Test Match Special in June 2020, but no doubt his distinctive style and voice will continue to be heard somewhere.

To end on an amusing footnote to the story of the 100th hundred, I want to briefly relate Jonathan Agnew's commentary box wind up which had Geoff Boycott hook line and sinker. The context of the wind up is that the 40th anniversary of the 100th hundred was just a few days away in 2017, and Aggers very cleverly produced an ICC press release on headed paper when live in the commentary box with Geoffrey at his side as co-commentator.

The press release concerned an England Test series in 1970, the one already mentioned by me earlier, this being the series against the Rest of the World, and it stated that on the request of the South African government, the ICC would now downgrade all statistics including runs and wickets from this series, and that all matches would subsequently be removed from first class records.

On air, and whilst Aggers continued commentary, Boycott called the decision ridiculous and a load of old tripe. Aggers went on to point out that if the 100 Geoffrey scored in this series was expunged, then this would mean that his cherished 100th hundred was not then the landmark 100 at Headingley in August 1977, rather it would be the next one, which was a first class 100 at the start of a tour of Pakistan in Faisalabad. Boycott's face is a picture, as he calls the ICC idiots, only for the hitherto dead pan Aggers to stand up and call it a wind up, to which Geoffrey responded "you muppet Agnew – he's done me like a kipper."

Chapter 3
The Boy from Pedrena

Friday 20th July 1979 –
Royal Lytham and St. Annes Golf Club

Golf has played a big part in my family history from the 1890s to the present day, and I have inherited the golf bug through both paternal and maternal genes. On my paternal side, my grandfather was a scratch golfer in the 1920s and 1930s at the outstanding Hollinwell Golf Club, also known as the North Notts Golf Club. It is an absolute gem of an inland course chiselled out of the north Nottinghamshire coalfields and has staged many important tournaments, and a course I have been privileged to play on many occasions.

Still on my paternal side, my other great grandfather was also a very handy golfer. He played his golf firstly at Ravenscliffe Golf Club in Eccleshill, Bradford (founded 1894), but after the First World War, the club was disbanded, and he moved to Bradford Golf Club (also known as Hawksworth Golf Club). He became Yorkshire Amateur Champion winning the final at Fixby Golf Club in 1902, apparently aided by his decision to play with the new longer flying ball, which his opponent declined, the newly invented rubber Haskell from the United States.

As the story was related in WP Wightman's obituary, apparently a team from Ravenscliffe Golf Club toured Ireland earlier that year, and found that the tee-shots of their opponents were consistently longer than their own. The mystery was later explained when they saw the new class of ball being used, and by some means or other one of the visiting team, Billy Smith, acquired a few of these new balls, and shortly afterwards and when WP Wightman and Douglas Gaunt met in the Yorkshire final, he produced the new rubber-core Haskell ball for both to trial. Whilst Mr Gaunt declared the new ball to be too lively, particularly on the greens, Mr Wightman decided to risk it, and not only played the first Haskell ball in the Yorkshire Amateur Championship, but won with it.

On my maternal side, the golfing genes were definitely Scottish, as my grandfather's family were originally from Dumfries and Galloway. They moved to Bradford in the early 1900s, and my grandfather played firstly at Bradford Moor Golf Club, and then later at Bradford Golf Club, and had a best handicap of five. My mother and her brother were both also single figure golfers, both brought up in a house which backed onto Bradford Moor Golf Club, and my mother and father in effect met each other through golf, and the rest you could say is history. I hasten to add that I am by some margin NOT the best golfer our family has produced, and with a best handicap of eight over 30 years ago, I would describe myself as an above average golfer. Even after 50 years, and now that my team sport playing days are over, golf is the game that still gets the competitive juices flowing, and I hope will continue to do so for many more years to come.

Early influences are evidently key factors in developing a love of sport, and if you combine this with opportunity, often great sportsmen emerge. They are born like anyone else, but if they are born into a golfing family, or they are brought up near a golf club, or perhaps they take up a role as a caddie at an early age, or have an obsessive father or coach as well, as in the case of Tiger Woods for example, who was handed his first golf club at the age of three, then all things are possible.

To emphasise this point I would recommend you read Mark Frost's book, The Greatest Game Ever Played, which recounts the remarkable true story of the 1913 US Open, which had at the heart of it, two main protagonists, the very experienced multi-major winning professional English golfer, Harry Vardon, himself born next to a golf course in Jersey, and the American Amateur golfer and former caddie, Francis Ouimet, brought up opposite the 15th fairway at Brookline Golf Club, which coincidentally just happened to be the venue for the 1913 US Open.

This particular entry into my 15 Great Sporting Memoirs tells the tale of a golfer of humble origins who was largely self-taught and who single handedly wrestled back from the Americans a European momentum which was to inspire fellow Europeans to great deeds and eighteen major championships in a twenty year period from 1979 to 1999. In this period, all these major wins were coincidentally achieved either at the Open or the US

Masters, though subsequently European golfers have now won the US Open and US PGA championships as well.

Severiano Ballesteros Sota was born on the 9th April 1957 in a small village called Pedrena, in Cantabria, northern Spain, just two miles across the bay from the large ferry port of Santander. What makes Seve's story so compelling is that his mother and father were of very humble origins, both were farm labourers working on a dairy farm, and they had five sons, of which Seve was the youngest. Although one died in childhood, remarkably of the four surviving sons, Baldomero, Vicente, Manuel and Seve all became professional golfers.

This may seem an unlikely turn of events, but there were two very important factors in the development of this family's connection with golf. Firstly, on Seve's maternal side, his uncle, Ramon Sota Ocejo was also a professional golfer of significant note, and good enough to finish 7th behind New Zealander Bob Charles in the 1963 Open at Royal Lytham and St Annes, and 5th in the 1965 US Masters which was won by Jack Nicklaus.

But by far the most important factor, was that despite there being very few golf clubs of note on the north coast of Spain, one of the best just happened to be in Pedrena itself. Real Golf de Pedrena is located on a small wooded peninsula and is a 1928 Harry Colt design classic, which affords stunning views from many of the greens across the Bay of Santander. To give you an idea of where Pedrena ranks as a golf course, if Real Valderrama is ranked the No. 1 course in Spain, Pedrena is currently ranked the 21st, and the equivalent here in the UK would be being born next to either Royal Troon or North Berwick in Scotland, or Royal Lytham and St Annes or St Enodoc in England.

Pedrena was therefore the quiet backwater that Seve was brought up in, and with older brothers to look up to, all of whom had already shown an interest in golf, and with a Championship golf course on his doorstep, perhaps it was no surprise what happened next. Seve was a most reluctant school boy as well, and this led to an altercation with his teacher, and expulsion, which allowed the young dreamer more time to self-practice, which was another key factor in accelerating his golf education, as well as honing his own brilliant shot making capabilities.

By this time, Seve's brothers had gifted him his first golf club, a wooden shafted 3 iron, with which he spent hours hitting balls, imagining shots and grooving his swing. By day he would caddie at Royal Pedrena, and then he would sneak onto the course at any opportunity, even into the wee hours under moonlit skies if the urge took him. By his own admission, Seve was obsessed with the game, and in the formative years from age 9 to 15, he would spend hours watching older golfers, like his uncle and his brothers, and at every chance he would hit golf balls, for hour after hour in the field behind his house where he designed his own golf course, using a tomato tin for a hole. Undoubtedly his passion for the game, and his ingenuity for shot making, born out of self-taught instinct and feel, were formulated in these exploratory and carefree years, and were the platform for what would be a golfing career like no other.

As good as caddying was for his pocket, at the going rate of

25 pesetas per round plus tips, Seve quickly realized that he was far more interested in playing, a fact which was also noted by one of Pedrena's more benevolent members, Dr Santiago, who invited him out to play with him and his friends. It didn't take long for Seve's precocious talent to develop, and he first won the annual caddies championship in 1970 as a 13 year old, and despite this being his only outlet for competition, Seve turned professional just before his 17th birthday in 1974.

Perhaps Royal Pedrena's greatest moment came in 1975 when it staged the Under 25 Spanish Championships, and with many of his family and friends putting money on Seve to win, the young 17 year old matador did not let his supporters down, running out an impressive victor, whilst demonstrating that along with the advantage of local knowledge, he possessed four very important qualities which would serve him well throughout his career, these being passion, belief, a competitive nature and a deep rooted desire to win.

It was now time for Seve to make his mark beyond the limiting borders of northern Spain, and it didn't take him long to announce himself on the world stage. Seve's elder brother Manuel was still playing on the European Tour with some success, but took on the dual role of player and Seve's manager. With his brother now looking after all off-course administration, young Seve was free to concentrate on practising and playing golf.

This allowed Seve his first taste of Open Championship golf, as both qualified for the 1975 Open, which was played at what is widely regarded to be the hardest of all Open venues, Carnoustie. Neither of the brothers starred, both missing the cut with Manuel shooting 75 and 76, and Seve eight shots worse with a 79 and an 80, but no doubt the experience was invaluable for the young Seve.

Another player making his Open debut that year was Tom Watson, and he was to fare rather better than Seve, taking the Claret Jug at the first time of asking following a play-off victory against Australian Jack Newton. Jack Newton was to suffer a career ending accident in 1983 when he lost his arm in a plane propeller, but Seve and Tom would go on to enjoy a great rivalry on the golf course over the next 20 years, which would see them win 13 Major tournaments between them.

The 1976 Open was played at Royal Birkdale. The long hot summer had left the fairways parched and the greens far from their best, but this week in the Southport dunes would prove to be Ballesteros' launching pad to stardom, and though ultimately he finished second to the brilliant Johnny Miller, no one doubted that the nineteen year old from Spain would one day be a major winner. And just who was this fresh faced, good looking, smiling, skinny Spaniard who was leading the Open by two shots after the second round?

Despite a tough day for scoring, Seve showed in the 3rd round that he was anything but overawed, and retained his two shot lead with a one over par 73, which meant he would go out in the last pairing with the 1973 US Open Champion Jonny Miller for the final round. On the final day,

Seve struggled with his driving, and a triple bogey on the 11th finally took him out of contention, allowing Miller to pull clear with an eagle at the 13th to win by six shots, after a fine final round of 66.

But Seve rallied in great style over the last six holes, finishing with an eagle of his own at the 17th, and a miraculous up and down at the last to save par which secured a tie for 2nd place with Jack Nicklaus. Having missed the 18th green by some distance to the left, Seve was short sided and it looked likely that he would make five and slip into third place, but having walked from his ball to the green, and carefully studied the bumpy and parched terrain, he displayed that already uncanny instinct and feel, forged on the beaches of Pedrena, to play the most outrageous pitch and run between two greenside bunkers to finish three feet from the flag.

A few weeks after the excitement of the Open, Seve won for the first time on the European Tour at the Dutch Open, and this would be the first of 90 victories on the international circuit. In the same year Seve closed with a back nine of 31 to overtake Arnold Palmer to win the Lancome Trophy, and after making his Masters debut in 1977, he returned in 1978 to win his first tournament in the States, shooting a final round 66 to secure the Greater Greensboro Open.

The following week he impressed many of the big names at Augusta, including playing partners Tom Weiskopf and Jack Nicklaus, both praising his effortless smooth swing and his long driving. Attacking courses with the charismatic aggression that Arnold Palmer had brought to the PGA 20 years previously certainly impressed David Feherty: "You knew you were in the presence of something special. There was sort of a feline grace to everything he did, kind of an animal like quality. You felt like he could change the weather with his mood. He would be thunderous one minute, his face would be purple, and when he smiled, the whole world lit up. A caddie who came from nothing, he just transformed European Golf, dragging it into the modern era the same way that Palmer did in America".

Seve was now making waves on both sides of the Atlantic, but despite another strong start in the Open at St Andrews, he followed his opening 69 and 70 with disappointing rounds of 76 and 73 to fall away over the weekend. He did however secure a respectable top 20 finish, and this experience of the Old Course, and all its quirks, as well as watching how Jack Nicklaus won his third and last Open Championship victory, would improve invaluable.

Thursday July 19th 1979 was an exciting day in my life, because it was my debut visit to an Open Championship, and as a fast improving 16 year old golfer, with all the enthusiasm to match, I was really looking forward to a day out with Dad. We were up early, and no doubt Mum packed us off with a hearty breakfast, and a substantial packed lunch, and according to my diary entry, we left home at 7.45am, and it takes c 2 hours to get across from Baildon to Lytham, so I guess we were on the course for about 10am.

These days the crowds at the Open are far bigger than they were back then. Including the practice days, nearly 240,000 fans attended at Royal Portrush last year, so approximately

50,000 per day on each of the 4 playing days, and the figure for July 19th 1979 was 28,250 … still a huge number of people, and crowds were not as effectively marshalled as they are today, nor were there as many stands around the course, so spectators had to fend for themselves, push and shove and run, and jockey for position if you wanted to watch the big names.

I vividly remember running and straining to get the best vantage points possible, something my father rarely had to do as he was 6 foot 5 inches tall! Spectators were carrying steps to stand on, shooting sticks, or carrying binoculars, and back in the 70s the golf mirror periscopes were very popular. Of course everyone wanted to see the big names, and we did get to see most of the leading contenders including two time winner Tom Watson who shot an impressive 68, Hale Irwin who was setting the pace on his way to back to back bogey free 68s, and the half-way lead, and also the ubiquitous Golden Bear himself, defending champion Jack Nicklaus.

Good advice when heading to the Open: get yourself an order of play sheet, and decide early on who you want to follow, and try and get ahead of the main crowds by positioning yourself early, perhaps at a good vantage point where you can see more than one hole. Thankfully we chose wisely and elected to follow Seve Ballesteros, and once again he didn't let his fans down. Having opened with a 73, which was eight shots behind Bill Longmuir, and five shots behind Hale Irwin, Seve needed a big round to get into contention, and was out in 33, with three consecutive birdies at the 6th, 7th and 8th holes.

As you can imagine, and given his growing reputation, there were plenty of people already following Seve, and his pairing with two time fast talking champion Lee Trevino added to the attraction too. We managed to catch up with Seve at the 13th hole, and were lucky enough to be able to follow him in. Having dropped shots at the 9th and 10th, things suddenly got supercharged again when a birdie putt dropped on the 14th, and then a chip in on the tricky 15th. Ironically it was the 16th hole, the easiest hole on the back nine, where Ballesteros did not birdie, missing from five foot, but he made up for this with a birdie following a stunning two iron approach at the difficult 17th, and then produced a breathtaking short iron at the last off a hanging lie to finish with another birdie, thereby equalling Longmuir's course record of 65.

I remember feeling exhilarated by what I had just seen, and sub-consciously inspired to get back on my own course as soon as possible to try a few things out. From that day I always had a soft spot for Seve, so he certainly was one of my boyhood heroes. I think this is the real essence of being there and seeing and hearing history being made in front of your very eyes. I suppose in hindsight this was even more exciting for me because Seve was not much older than I was, and the exuberance of youth and the sheer joy of watching the adrenalin flow as he played in such a carefree cavalier fashion was infectious. Along with the hordes, Dad and I were propelled breathlessly along, cheers all around us and in the distance too, as and when the news of Seve's charge reached other scoreboards on the course.

Another great aspect of watching the Open Championship, and especially if you go to watch either of the first or second rounds is that you get great value for money, and if you choose to, and if the weather stays fair, you can watch golf from 6.30am in the morning, to 8pm at night. We certainly watched lots of other matches on the day, as my diary entry says we didn't get home until 9.40pm. What a day out! At the end of the day, Hale Irwin led by two shots, from Ballesteros, with Tom Watson two shots further back, and Jack Nicklaus a shot further back, and all was set for an exciting weekend.

Blustery conditions on England's West Coast would dominate over the final two days of competition, which ensured the field tightened together, and as both Irwin and Ballesteros took 75, Nicklaus, Crenshaw, and particularly Mark James with a fine 69 were all within touching distance. If Seve's swashbuckling 65 on Day 2 put him into contention, he still needed to deliver another outstanding round to win his first major, and there were plenty of very good players waiting for him to slip up.

As the difficult squally conditions prevailed, Seve's final round 70 was one of only four scores under par. He stuck to his game plan which saw him play with a mixture of courage, misplaced bravado, aggression, even willfulness, hurling himself at every tee shot, and finding the rough with nine of his tee-shots in the final round. He may well have benefited from some kindly trampled down lies, but he also hit some brilliant recovery shots, and relied heavily on his touch around the greens, out of bunkers, and of course with his putter when on the greens.

In the final straight, it was his play over the last six holes that typified all his qualities. At the 13th he drove into a bunker, at the 14th and 15th he drove into the rough, first right, and then left, and right again on the 16th where he found a car park, and then at the treacherous 17th he was in the rough again, in the bunker in two, but on all occasions he saved par. Whilst the most memorable image of Seve's final round for many of us is his taking a free drop in the car park away from a white Ford Escort, far more importantly, and surely a sign of greatness, he followed up his good break with a crisply struck short iron into the heart of the green, and a perfectly weighted putt into the heart of the hole for an inevitable birdie, which in effect put him beyond the reach of his closest pursuers.

He still needed to avoid the out of bounds at the back of the 18th which is an unusual characteristic of Royal Lytham, and this might explain why his approach shot after another pulled drive, was for the first time relatively and surprisingly conservative. Or you could say that it was clear evidence that even at a time of such pressure, he was still in total command of his emotions. It came up five yards short of the green, and clear of the first greenside bunker on the left. But it merely resulted in a dead weight putt from 60 feet or so, leaving Seve a tap in and a victory by three clear shots from two Americans, Jack Nicklaus and Ben Crenshaw.

Earlier in the week Ballesteros had said in an interview: "We should play British Open without fairways, then I come close to win." After the victory, with his three brothers weeping with joy he added, "I don't aim for the rough, it just goes there. My caddie tell me to close the eyes and hit it. Maybe I go into the fairway". The facts are that with driver in hand, Seve hit only nine fairways in 72 holes that week, and on the final day just one, so in effect he had played and won the Open without fairways after all, which just goes to show how great his powers of recovery were.

As Seve's career blossomed, it became abundantly clear that his game was far more suited to the more open terrains offered up by links golf and also by the relatively wide fairways that characterised Augusta National. Whereas a wayward drive would often get badly penalised at the US Open for example, links courses and Augusta allowed mistakes, and because Seve had such instinct and touch around the greens, he could get up and down from most places. It is therefore no great surprise that all five of his Majors came at the Open or at Augusta.

At 22 years old, Seve was the youngest winner of the Open since Tom Morris Junior, who won his first Open in 1868 at 17 years old, and his 4th and final Open in 1872 at 21 years old, and the first Continental European winner since Frenchman Arnaud Massey in 1907. The following year, he would take Augusta by storm to become at 23 years old the youngest winner of the Green Jacket, a record which stood until Tiger Woods won his first Augusta title in 1997 at 21 years old.

By now Seve was a household name on both sides of the Atlantic, and had even made his debut appearance in the 1979 Ryder Cup which was held in America, and which Europe lost 17-11. Seve would miss the 1981 return match played at Walton Heath because of an ongoing dispute about appearance money, which seems at odds with his obvious love affair with the event, which then saw him play in seven consecutive Ryder Cups from 1983 to 1995.

Back in 1976 Jack Nicklaus had seen the impact of Seve Ballesteros at Royal Birkdale, and had been the main driver for widening the appeal of the Ryder Cup to include Continental Europe, and Seve became Europe's talisman for the next two decades. As a result the Ryder Cup was revived, and ever since matches have been regularly very closely fought contests, as illustrated by the results from eight of the nine matches played between 1983 and 1999, which were all won by wafer thin margins of no more than two points.

Seve's Ryder Cup record was one of the best, and he and fellow Spaniard Jose Maria Olazabal boast the best record of any pairing, having played 15 times together, chalking up 11 victories, two halves and only two defeats across Foursomes and Fourball competition. Seve was an inspiration to his team mates, and often an awkward opponent for the Americans.

Olazabal made his Ryder Cup debut in 1987 at Muirfield Village, and as his then caddie Billy Foster recalls overhearing in the afternoon fourball match against Tom Kite and Curtis Strange, Seve was keen to protect his younger charge, saying on the first fairway "I will take care of these sons of bitches, you listen to me". When Seve then missed the green with his approach shot, he asked Jose to putt first, so Seve could have a free run at his chip for birdie.

Olazabal's putt went some distance by, and Seve asked him to hole out for a par, but Strange took it upon himself to say that he might be standing on his line. Seve stormed off to his chip, and played it deftly right into the hole for a birdie, and then walked across the green right up to Strange and bellowed in his ear "Any problems now Curtis?"

This was typical of Seve's competitive nature. Never prepared to stand down, take a backward step, or to believe he could not win from any situation, he was a force of nature. He would still produce these amazing shots, which famously also included him taking on the par four 10th at the Belfry, carrying the water, and landing on the green, leaving an eagle putt. He surely had a presence, which must have had a massive psychological impact on even the toughest of opponents.

Perhaps his proudest Ryder Cup moment was the 1997 match played for the first time in Spain, at Valderrama, for which Seve was appointed non-playing captain. The first two days went very much to plan for Europe, and they led 10.5 to 5.5 points going into the final day singles. The Americans responded brilliantly as one by one the European big guns lost their matches, and although Europe only need four points to retain the trophy, no one was quite sure where the points would come from.

Seve had packed his bottom half with big names, including Olazabal, Langer, Westwood, Montgomerie, Faldo – but only Bernard Langer could record a victory, which had Seve careering around on his buggie, even appearing to try and play some of the shots himself. Thankfully Colin

Montgomerie's nerve held long enough, and realising that it was all on his shoulders from the 16th fairway, and fearing what Seve's reaction would be if he didn't pull through, he bravely secured that crucial half point which gifted Seve the coveted Ryder Cup win on his home soil.

Back to major golf, Seve would win his second Green Jacket in 1983 by the convincing margin of four shots again, and in 1984 he would capture his second Open victory, after an epic tussle with five time champion Tom Watson. Watson had won both the Open and US Open in 1982, and the Open again at Royal Birkdale in 1983, and was hoping to equal Harry Vardon's record with a third consecutive win at the home of golf.

Watson shot a third round 66 to hit the top of the leader board with Ian Baker-Finch, with Seve two shots further back on nine under par, but it all came down to the dreaded 17th Road Hole, where Watson's approach to the kidney shaped green went long, and ended up by the back wall. His bogey there, and Seve's fist pumping birdie at the 18th, along with that broad beaming smile and guttural roar are abiding images for all of Seve's many supporters.

After his victory at St Andrew's there were back to back disappointments at Augusta for Seve. In 1986 he had victory in his grasp, having just eagled the 13th to go three shots clear, but an uncharacteristic mistake on the par five 15th led to a bogey, and Jack Nicklaus then produced an amazing back nine of 30 shots, which included an eagle at the 15th, and birdies at the 16th and 17th to edge home from Kite, Norman and Ballesteros, all of whom could have won. Seve would also just miss out in 1987, when he lost in a three way play off which included Greg Norman and Larry Mize, the latter winning with a Seve like chip in on the 10th hole.

Undoubtedly Seve was most at home at Augusta, where he had seven top five finishes, and looking back at his career, perhaps five Major victories were not quite the due reward for the style of golf he played, and the charisma and joy that he brought to so many. There was however to be one more Major triumph for Seve, and this rather appropriately would come in 1988 at the venue where he won his first major, Royal Lytham.

Seve got off to a great start with an exciting 67 on Thursday, a score which was matched in the second round by half-way leader Nick Price. After heavy rain led to the abandonment of Saturday's play, the 3rd round was played on Sunday, and it saw Nick Price extend his lead by two shots over Ballesteros and Faldo, and the final day was for the first time played on a Monday, and it saw a brilliant display of golf as Price and Ballesteros outplayed Faldo, and matched each other shot for shot, birdie for birdie.

Just as the 16th had been kind to Seve in 1979, so it was again, a cast iron regulation birdie this time from the middle of the fairway, and as they went to the 18th tee, it was just this shot that separated the two. When Seve missed the green with his approach, Price saw his opportunity, albeit he had a long 45 foot putt for birdie. But what followed next was a moment of pure Seve genius, as he produced a near perfect pitch from an awkward lie which all but went in. Price had a dart at his putt which went some distance by and Seve was Open Champion again.

"That was the best round of my life" said Seve, and when interviewed afterwards by Harry Carpenter, Seve wanted to put the record on 1979 straight when many described him rather unfairly as the car park champion. " First of all, I'd just like to say it's pity I didn't find any cars on the 16th fairway this time. Unfortunately the R and A should park their cars on the fairway next time because I am becoming a very straight player now".

So five Major victories, six European Tour Order of Merits, five World Match Play titles, 90 professional titles in all, and of course that amazing Ryder Cup record. Seve's golfing career was incredible, and so was his shot-making capability, and no summary is complete without mentioning that miracle shot in the last round at the last hole at the 1993 European Masters at the spectacular Swiss course, Crans-sur-Sierre Montana. Shunning the advice of caddie Billy Foster, and still very much in contention, Seve produced a miracle eye of the needle recovery shot through dense foliage and over a wall, and then chipped in at the 18th for a sixth consecutive grandstand birdie finish.

No one else could have played that shot, because no one else could have imagined it. And to me, and apart from what I witnessed at Royal Lytham as an impressionable 16 year old, that is Seve's real legacy.

The Seve story has a tragic ending, because after everything he gave to the World of Golf, and following the announcement of his retirement in 2007, the bright light that was Seve was suddenly extinguished when he died of brain cancer at the very young age of 54 on May 7th 2011. As I write this paragraph, coincidentally today would have been Seve's 63rd birthday, and perhaps more important to him, it would also have been the first round of the 2020 Masters tournament at his beloved Augusta.

Ever popular with the British public, Seve was awarded the BBC Sports Personality Lifetime Achievement Award for the second time in 2009, which was appropriately presented to him by his great friend, compatriot and Ryder Cup team mate Jose Maria Olazabal at his home in Pedrena. Seve's lecacy continues not just through the memory of his amazing golf shots, and not just through that big smile and swagger of his but also through the Seve Ballesteros Foundation which aims to research cancer, especially brain tumours.

A passionate genius with a unique talent, of all the tributes paid to Seve at the time of his death, I have picked out two. The first is by Bernard Gallacher who was Ryder Cup captain from 1991-1995. "Every European Tour player should thank Seve for what they're playing for. America had Jack Nicklaus and Arnold Palmer – Seve was our Arnold Palmer and Jack Nicklaus rolled into one. You can't speak too highly of him, Seve was Europe's best ever player"

The second tribute is from the other side of the Atlantic, and comes from America's own recovery shot specialist, Phil Mickelson. Mickelson had hoped that Seve would be able to make his regular appearance at the 2011 Past Champions dinner, which traditionally takes place on the

Tuesday evening of Masters week. As is customary, the current champion, Mickelson, would be expected to choose the menu, but on hearing that Seve was too ill to travel, he went against tradition and instead honoured his hero by serving a Spanish dish.

Seve was destined to have the last laugh the following year, when the European Ryder Cup team, captained by Jose Maria Olazabal, were staring down defeat in the biennial match which was being played at the Medinah Country Club, Illinois. The Americans took a 10-6 lead into the Sunday singles, and but for the heroics of Ian Poulter, their lead could have been significantly more. A few hours later, the scoreboard was blue, and Europe took the singles eight and a half to three and a half, to win 14 and a half to 13 and a half. Quickly labelled as "the Miracle at Medinah" a highly emotional and tearful Jose Maria looked up to the skies to thank Seve for his inspiration, with the Spanish papers reporting the following day that "This one is for you Seve."

Chapter 4
The Miracle of Headingley

16th -21st July 1981

The family tradition of always going to day one and day three of the Headingley Test match did not always mean that you got to see the most exciting part of the match. In 1977, I had been fortunate in that Boycott produced his special day on the day I was there. In 1981, I was less fortunate because days one and three of the third Ashes Test at Headingley were, in all honesty, quite dull and remarkably unsuccessful from an England perspective. However, I had to include this match in this book, because I was there for large parts of it, and it was one of, if not the greatest ever, sporting turnarounds. It was and still is exactly as Richie Benaud described it when the last Australian wicket fell on that fateful Tuesday afternoon: "That's one of the most fantastic victories ever known in Test cricket history".

The context to this match was that England had been on a very poor run of form, having gone twelve matches without a win since their triumph in the Golden Jubilee Test in Bombay (now Mumbai). All these matches had been played under the captaincy of Ian Botham who had emerged as one of England's best players and most charismatic characters, but as is often the case in sport, and for some reason particularly in cricket, accomplished match winning all-rounders do not necessarily turn into naturally gifted captains.

Many said at the time of his appointment that it was a mistake to appoint Botham as captain in the first place. Traditionally Test captains are often top order batsmen, sometimes spin bowlers, rarely fast bowlers or all rounders. All rounders tend to be in the game all the time and the added responsibility of being captain can end up being a burden. As happened to Botham, a loss of personal form, a loss of confidence with bat and ball, a swing in momentum to the other team, all were contributing factors in Ian Botham and England's case.

Hindsight is a wonderful thing, but history does have a habit of repeating itself. On the back of the extraordinary Ashes series win in 2005, Michael Vaughan was rightly hailed at the best captain in world cricket. His ensuing knee injury was unfortunate for both player and country in respect of the return Ashes series in Australia in 2006/7. The selectors, who in the meantime had trialled both Andrew Flintoff and Andrew Strauss as captains in Vaughan's absence, then made the same tactical error by appointing Flintoff as captain for the Ashes campaign.

The form of both players suffered for different reasons, Flintoff because he had too much responsibility, Strauss because he didn't have enough. The result was a humiliating 5-0 series defeat for Flintoff and England. The Australian public who hold Flintoff in high esteem for his cricketing deeds and engaging personality were genuinely disappointed to see the great man so diminished by the task and most questioned the thinking of the England selectors at the time.

Back to 1981, and the coveted Ashes were at stake and the first Test was staged at Trent Bridge, and in a low scoring contest, Australia triumphed by four wickets, heaping pressure on the England captain, who was now being offered the captaincy on a match by match basis. The Lords Test followed, and although it ended in a draw, with England slightly in the ascendancy, it had proved the last straw for Ian Botham, and for the England selectors. Botham recorded an ignominious pair, and was met with a wall of silence by the MCC members as he made his sorry way back from the middle. Botham fell on his sword, before the selectors pushed him, and Mike Brearley was hastily recalled to take on the captaincy for the remaining four Tests. The side he led into the 3rd Test at Headingley would include the outgoing captain, but how would Ian Botham react to losing the captaincy, and how would Brearley manage him?

Under grey skies on Thursday 16th July Australian captain Kim Hughes won the toss and chose to bat and on a rain curtailed day which produced fairly pedestrian cricket, Australia were in a strong position at 203/3 thanks to John Dyson's patient century. Australia batted for most of the second day too and 89 from skipper Kim Hughes, and 58 from Graham Yallop allowed Australia to declare at 401/9, England closing at 7/0 wicket. There had been one positive sign in the post tea session for England, when Botham had been given a long bowl and was rewarded in this spell with 5/35, taking an excellent 6/95 off 39.2 overs. Brearley was clearly trying to get his talisman back into form.

England had a nightmare third day that saw them skittled out for 174, and then were asked to follow on. The one positive note was a further glimpse of the former Ian Botham with bat in hand this time, as he top scored with exactly 50. Before the close, England had lost Graham Gooch for a duck to Dennis Lillee, and to round off a thoroughly miserable day for English supporters, the day ended in great controversy when umpires Don Oslear and Ken Palmer then took the players off the field early for bad light.

I remember very clearly the crowd reaction to this, as irate spectators threw their green and red hired seat cushions onto the outfield in disgust. There followed an increasingly ill-tempered stand off between large sections of the crowd and the umpires. This ended in uproar as the weather suddenly improved, but the umpires had already abandoned play for the night.

Thus a thoroughly despondent home crowd left the ground, mad at the umpires and frustrated at the impotence of the England team. It's difficult to know which team was done the greater disservice by the bizarre actions of the umpires, but most saw this as just a stay of execution for England's beleaguered players. England were 6/1 at the close, and still 221 runs behind on first innings, staring at defeat and even worse, a 2-0 series deficit with only three matches to play.

Sunday 19th July was a rest day in the Test, so at least England had a day to recharge, but so did the Australian quick bowlers, Dennis Lillee, Terry Alderman and Geoff Lawson, and no doubt this was a factor in Kim Hughes' thinking when he had asked England to follow on. There was very little talk about the Test match on the Sunday, and instead I made a diary entry which said that I had scored a useful if streaky 27 not out for the West Riding Cricket Club, before bowling out our opposition, Ben Rhydding Cricket Club, for 104. That was certainly far more important to me than what had been going on at Headingley.

So to be quite honest, the third day of this Test, indeed the first 3 days of this Test, were quite ordinary and very one sided, played under grey skies, and certainly from an England point of view, far from memorable. And yet, cricket being the strange game it sometimes can be, contrived over the next day and a half to produce one of the most memorable and always talked about Test matches of all time.

I watched day four unravel on television at home and for the most part it echoed the momentum of the first three days. Australia were still on top, driving home the advantage and their trio of fast bowlers were still bowling well, with spinner Ray Bright not even required to bowl. When the obdurate and hitherto unmoveable Geoff Boycott fell lbw to Terry Alderman after a stoic three and a half hour vigil which yielded him only 46 runs, England had slumped to 133/6, and when Bob Taylor quickly fell to the same bowler, England were 135/7, still 92 runs in arrears.

The Headingley crowd on that fourth day was understandably small and those who were watching at home were only watching small passages of play before doing something else. A short spell on the practice ground (interrupted by wind and rain) and an annoying wait in town as my younger sister had her ears pierced all seemed to be worthy distractions to the cricket, as my diary entry explains.

However, where there is life, there is hope, and when Ian Botham was joined by Graham Dilley, both decided to have some fun and started hitting themselves out of trouble. The diary goes on to say quite simply that Botham played the innings of his life but this statement completely underestimates the part that Dilley played in the recovery.

If anything, it was Dilley's carefree striking that initially sparked Botham into more serious action, and after tea, both began to take advantage of the flagging Australian quick bowlers, when the bat was thrown at anything short, wide or pitched up in their swinging arcs. Dilley's left handedness and powerful offside play was the perfect foil to Botham's all round shot making.

Botham was later to heap praise on Dilley who he said had matched him stroke for stroke. The two were enjoying batting together, oblivious of the match situation now, almost accepting of defeat, totally unrestrained in a way perhaps only bowlers can be when they bat, and trying to regain some respectability. Graham Dilley hit nine powerfully struck boundaries, including a glorious cover drive to reach his maiden Test 50, and suddenly England had passed their follow on target of 227.

Dilley was eventually bowled by Alderman attempting another big boundary, for a superb 56, and looking back at his Test statistics, this would prove to be the highest score of his career. Dilley and Botham had added an entertaining 117 for the 8th wicket, but at 252/8, England were still perilously placed, only 25 runs ahead, when Yorkshire's Chris Old joined Botham at the crease.

Much to the joy of the Yorkshire crowd, the left-handed Old carried on in the same vein as Dilley, crashing 6 boundaries of his own in a quick fire 29. At the other end, Botham was swinging himself off his feet and having a go at just about every ball, and reached if not the prettiest, surely one of the most brutal and entertaining 100s of his career. (This was his seventh Test century, scored off just 87 balls). One particular shot stands out for me, as much for the pureness of the strike, and in equal measure for Richie's Benaud's memorable commentary. Botham charged down the wicket to Alderman, and hit him cleanly over long on for 6, resulting in Benaud's perfectly timed comment in that enduring Australian twang of his: "Don't bother looking for that, never alone chasing it – it's gone straight into the confectionery stall and out again".

They added another priceless 67 runs before Geoff Lawson clean bowled Old. England had advanced to 319/9, 92 runs ahead, and as last man Bob Willis walked to the middle, skipper Mike Brearley was seen urging Botham to stay out there, to carry on playing his shots, and extend the lead. This may be the appropriate time to record due praise to England's

captain, because without his timely and acute man management skills, none of those lower order runs from particularly
Botham, but also Dilley and Old, or those eight wickets taken
by Willis might have happened. Only Mike Brearley could
have overseen such a rapid turn around in fortunes.

Botham and Willis stayed together for the rest of that
evening adding another 32 runs taking the score up to
351/9. Unbelievably in the space of two hours, England had
not only avoided the follow on, they had now stolen a lead
of 124 runs. What would be the mental state of the
Australian batsmen after such an onslaught? Could Botham
and Willis add another thirty or even fifty runs on the
following morning? Could England do what only one other
side had done in the history of Test match cricket, namely
win a match after following on?

You have to go back to the 1894/95 England tour of
Australia. In a match played at the SCG, Sydney, and in reply
to Australia's huge first innings of 586, England scored 325,
and following on, 437. Australia were 113/2 at the end of
the fourth day, needing another 63 to win, but after heavy
overnight rain, were dismissed for just 166, losing by 10
runs.

Since 1981, there has been one other example, a match
played at Eden Gardens, Kolkata, which also saw Australia
lose. Australia, having posted 445 in their first innings, went
on to dismiss India for 171. Following on, India made a
mammoth 657/7 declared in their second innings, VVS
Laxman scoring 281, and although Australia reached tea on
the final day at 161/3, the match seemingly petering out

to a draw, they would lose their last 7 wickets for 51 runs to lose by 171 runs.

Suddenly there was renewed interest in the match and the series. Day five got underway and England were only able to add a further five runs before Willis was caught by Border to give Alderman a sixth wicket in the innings. Ian Botham was left not out 149 and walked off the field to generous applause from the still sparse crowd, no longer the downcast villain we had seen at Lord's, now the returning fearless Fearnley wielding hero that we all loved.

Now that Australia's target had been set, the crowd swelled in number as workers in and around Bradford and Leeds sensed that an upset could be on the cards, and with only 130 needed to win, staff could in theory be back at their desks by early afternoon whatever the result. These were the happy days when you didn't have to pay for Sky Sports, and the good old BBC were there again, Christopher Martin-Jenkins, Tom Graveney, and the brilliant Richie Benaud to the fore, and I remember feeling very jealous when Dad came home that evening saying how lucky he had been to take a long lunch hour, and watch it all unfold that afternoon.

As any cricketer will tell you, chasing a low score at any level can be tricky. Fast bowlers have a new ball to work with, and know that there will probably be only two or three hours of play before a result, so they have nothing to lose. In contrast, batsmen may see this as an easy total to surpass, and may approach their task with an element of complacency, in the knowledge that if they fail, others will step up. I am yet to see a coaching manual that tells you exactly how a batting side will best reach a small target. Sides chasing small targets usually do win, but surprisingly less often than you think, and often only after having lost more wickets than expected. In this particular situation, there was also a psychological effect, because England had changed the momentum of the match, a match which had been lost, was now a match that was still alive, and could be won.

Everyone still expected Australia to win easily and although England were buoyed by the early wicket of Wood caught behind off who else but Ian Botham, the first innings centurion John Dyson played calmly and at 56/1 approaching lunch the Australians were in total control of their own destiny. Call it a captain's intuition, but Brearley played his masterstroke, changing Bob Willis to the Kirkstall Lane End where he had the wind at his back.

Willis was transformed and either side of lunch took eight Australian wickets in what can only be described as the best bowling performance of his life. Botham's heroics were not to be wasted, and they definitely inspired his team mate to fame and glory. As is often the case in these tight matches, there were also some very good catches taken, including a belter at second slip by Botham, two very low catches by Mike Gatting and a very well judged skier by Graham Dilley at fine leg, just inside the rope. The rout was completed by Willis as Ray Bright was clean bowled, dismissed for the ironic score of 111, and incredibly Australia had fallen 19 runs short of their target.

The look on Bob Willis' face throughout his spell (15.1 overs, 8/43) was trance like, mesmeric, almost demonic in its intensity. He suddenly found his rhythm, an extra yard of pace, and some very awkward bounce. On taking the last wicket, middle stump uprooted out of the ground as if to emphasise the result, I recall him running towards the pavilion, arms swinging with triumph, almost unaware of what he had achieved, leaving a trail of beaming team mates in his wake. It was one of those goal scorer moments; watch carefully next time you see a goal scorer celebrate, because more often than not it's the scorer who is back to the half way line for the restart before anyone else. Willis was the first back to the Headingley pavilion, vaulting up the steps to the balcony, as delirious supporters raced onto the pitch and closed in on him, and his fellow team mates.

An amusing footnote to these great deeds at Headingley was the soon to emerge story involving Ladbrokes the bookmakers. Having offered up odds of 500/1 on an England victory one or two speculators did rather well out of the situation. These included one well known Yorkshireman, Albert Geoffrey Parker, one of the famous Pudsey St Lawrence Parker cricketing clan. There were others who also took the bet on, and controversially these included two members of the losing team. Never one to miss out on a good thing, apparently fast bowling legend Dennis Lillee and wicket keeper Rodney Marsh saw the odds posted and couldn't believe it, although at the time things were hushed up pretty quickly for obvious reasons.

According to an interview in 1998, Lillee said he had never

seen such ludicrous odds for a two-horse race and announced to everyone in the dressing room that he was going to have a 100 quid on the rank outsider. His team mates said he was mad and demanded instead that he put the money on the bar at the end of the Test. So he sat down and didn't do anything about it, at least not then. Later, when England were 135/7, and the odds were still the same, he got the Australian team bus driver Peter to put a £10 stake on, and the rest is history as they say. Needless to say, I don't think we will ever see odds like that again!

This truly was a remarkable Test match and ultimately it was down to two players producing extraordinary performances in the same Test match. It is worth taking a moment to get the thoughts of Ian Botham and Bob Willis after it all happened.

Observing in his autobiography "Head On" published in 2007, Botham described events as follows: "Slowly, imperceptibly, the mood of the two teams changed. Graham and I were having the time of our lives, smiling and laughing in the middle of the wicket between overs but, from their expressions, the Australians weren't getting the joke at all. They were deadly serious now, but we were still carting them all over the ground. From the time we passed their total I can't remember playing a single defensive stroke. I hooked, pulled, cut and drove, and if I flashed, I flashed hard....I glanced up to the balcony at one point, expecting to see Mike Brearley urging restraint but instead he was miming even wilder and more extravagant strokes. I tried to oblige... My own favourite was a square cut off Dennis Lillee that cannoned off the boundary boards before any of the fielders had moved. Later on, and back in the dressing room I flopped down, put my feet up, lit a cigar and struggled to make sense of what had just happened, but I rapidly gave up trying".

And Bob Willis for his part later commented... "The Aussie skipper Kim Hughes just had the fielders in the wrong positon and wouldn't bowl Ray Bright for some reason...I was actually fourth choice bowler in the second innings and never enjoyed bowling from the Football Stand end, so asked Brearley to change ends to the Kirkstall Lane End". Peter West's interview on the day of the match was interesting... and when talking about the key over just before lunch when he claimed the wickets of Yallop and Hughes, Willis said in his familiar deadpan way "I told Mike I was a bit too old to be bowling into the wind, so I better bowl at the other end".

The series was now tied at 1-1 with three Tests remaining, but England never looked back from this point, the momentum shift was palpable, winning the fourth and fifth Tests to seal the series even before the final Test. For the record Botham transformed the fourth Test at Edgbaston with the ball just as emphatically as he had with the bat at Headingley. England looked doomed to defeat after totalling 189 and 219 against the swing of Alderman and the spin of Bright. In a match in which no batsman reached 50, Australia just required 151 to win, surely lightning could not strike again?

Australia were well placed at 87/3 at one stage, but Brearley managed to persuade Botham, who had been initially reluctant, to have a go, and the Australian middle and lower order collapsed, losing their last six wickets for just 16 runs in the space of just 47 minutes, Botham producing an inspired spell to capture the last five wickets for just one run.

Two weeks later the action had moved to Old Trafford where the two sides met again for the Fifth Test, and the Australians must have been delighted to restrict England to 231 all out, and particularly pleased when Dennis Lillee got Botham out first ball.

Very quickly the Australians were in trouble though, with Headingley heroes Willis and Botham picking up seven wickets between them, as they helped dismiss the old enemy for a paltry 130 runs in just 30.2 overs. Australia were still in the game when they had reduced England in their second innings to 104/5, but this brought Botham to the crease, and he changed the game again in the space of 100 minutes, scoring a breathtaking 118 off 102 balls.

If Botham's Headingley knock had been brutal and ungainly, he set the record straight here with what most observers describe as the best innings of his life. Hitting six sixes and thirteen fours in all, this was a chanceless innings that had everything – timing, stroke play all around the ground, courage, entertainment and gravitas, in that it pointed England towards a third consecutive Test victory to secure the series. The final Sixth Test of the series at the Oval ended as a draw, Border and Boycott scoring centuries, Botham picking up 10 more wickets, whilst Dennis Lillee returned career best bowling figures of 11/159.

Momentum is a great thing to have in life and in sport in particular. At the start of the series England were devoid of luck, leadership and couldn't buy a win from anywhere. However, a change of leadership, and one heroic innings in combination with a match winning bowling performance brought about a rapid and unstoppable shift of fortunes. Beware the wounded player. In this instance it was Botham's pride that had been wounded. It takes something special to alter momentum so dramatically, and that's precisely what happened in this series. Single Tests are often dubbed after players, but the 1981 series has gone down in history as "Botham's Ashes", and it was an Ashes momentum that England would maintain over Australia until 1989.

I don't know what the television viewing figures were for this remarkable series, but given that they were available on terrestrial TV, I am sure Botham's Ashes inspired a generation of youngsters to play cricket and even for the already converted, which included this 18 year old, three words in my diary entry for Tuesday 21st July "oiled my bat" (which was also a Duncan Fearnley) suggests that I too was very much inspired by the heroics of IT Botham.

The other effect it had on me was to put pen to paper, in the form of a rhyming poem, which I boldly delivered by hand for the attention of the then head of the TMS commentary team, former Glamorgan and England captain, Tony Lewis. Here is my Headingley poem, for which I would later receive an acknowledgement and thanks from the BBC. (See page 132).

Testing Time...

Watching that Headingley Test
I saw cricket at its best
Australia had a first innings lead
Which England might not supercede.

Our hopes for the series were in doubt,
For the tail would soon be all out.
But Botham came to the wicket,
And began to play real cricket

Iron Botham, built like a steel buttress,
Slashed ball with bat with his cutlass,
6's over long on, 4's over slip,
As his bat flayed like a whip.

Despite the might of Dennis Lillee,
100 to Botham and 50 to Dilley.
Botham continued his onslaught,
Old assisted before being caught.

On the final day Willis was soon gone,
But Botham had been there all along,
Cheered by all, the sun did shine,
Botham retired, not out 149.

Australia had an easy task,
But those runs, each wore a mask.
Things went slowly and then before lunch,
Big Bob came in with the crunch.

As he roared into the Australian batting,
Yallop went, well caught by Gatting.
It still seemed England would lose
But in the same over they lost Kim Hughes.

Aussies 4 down at the break,
6 wickets left, but a few runs to make.
English hearts grew weak and then proud,
Dyson ct Taylor b Willis saw the crowd.

The Aussies still had the in-form Border,
A stubborn defence in their middle order.
But he too fell deservedly to Old,
Through the gate, clean bowled.

An English victory was now in sight,
But there followed a rearguard by Lillee and Bright.
Tension grew in the greatest of matches,
It got to Old, when he dropped 2 catches.

Then Gatting leapt in and Lillee was out,
And Big Bob completed the rout.
Bright, Lawson, Alderman all went the same.
To Willis, 8 for 43, and eternal fame.

Chapter 5
Only a 4 to win the Open!

Royal Birkdale: 112th Open Championship
Sunday 10th to Sunday 17th July 1983

For golf fans all over the world, the Open Championship has a special place in their hearts. It is the oldest of golf's four Majors, and the only one played in the UK and is uniquely always played on a links golf course. A links is the oldest style of golf course, first developed in Scotland, and the term is typically associated with coastal courses, often amid dunes, where water hazards and trees are rarities. By the very nature of the locations of the links courses that comprise the Open rota, both terrain and weather are often a determining factor in the outcome of the championship.

Scotland is therefore the natural home of golf and the first Open was staged at Prestwick Golf Club in 1860 and was won by Willie Park, with Tom Morris Senior winning the second Open in 1861. Two of the biggest names in Open history, the Park and Morris families would go on to win no fewer than thirteen of the first fifteeen Opens played. Home of the Royal and Ancient Golf Club, St Andrews first staged the Open in 1873 and will stage the 150th Open Championship in 2022. The oldest winner of the Open was Tom Morris Senior, also known as Old Tom Morris, in 1867 (46 years and 102 days), and his son Tom Morris Junior was the youngest winner at 17 years and 156 days old when he won the first of his four consecutive Open titles in 1868.

The first Englishman to win the Open was John Ball in 1890, and the first course to stage the Open outside of Scotland was Royal St Georges, Sandwich, Kent, in 1894, and it was at this Open that John Henry Taylor, who played his golf at Royal North Devon, perhaps better known as Westward Ho!, won the first of five Open titles. "JHT" was one part of the Great Triumvirate of pioneer professional golfers, which also included Jersey's Harry Vardon, and Scotland's James Braid.

Having fought out many battles on golf courses far and wide over a 20 year period, when the Triumvirate teed up at Prestwick Golf Club in the summer of 1914 to compete in the 54th Open Championship, they were reaching the twilight of their careers, but remarkably each had won five Open Titles. The Great War would then interrupt their careers, and by the time the Open restarted after five long years in 1920, younger men were making their mark.

Although they were unaware at the time of the true significance of this Open, one of the Great Triumvirate was about to etch their name in the golfing record books for ever. Braid could only finish in a tie for 10th, but Vardon and Taylor were difficult to separate, and it was Taylor who led by two shots going into the final round. Paired together, and in front of huge crowds, the two battled it out again one last time, Vardon taking the lead at the fourth with a par to Taylor's triple bogey seven, and the Jerseyman never looked back and prevailed by three shots to win a sixth Open title, a tally which to this day has not been matched.

The first US Open was staged in 1895, and was for the early years dominated by pioneering Scots who had crossed the Atlantic to make their fortunes. Harry Vardon also made that long boat trip to compete in and win the 1900 US Open, a victory which in hindsight was a catalyst for golf to become the global sport it is today. American amateur golfer Bobby Jones took the world by storm in the 1920s, and won all four Majors in 1930, and he and fellow American Walter Hagen dominated the Open in the 1920s.

The Americans then fell out of love with the Open and in the 1950s and 1960s an Australian, Peter Thompson, also won five Opens, including three consecutive titles from 1954-56, and it took the charisma of Arnold Palmer who won the Open in 1961 and 1962 to rekindle American interest, since when Jack Nicklaus and Tiger Woods have each won the Open on three occasions.

However, when it comes to American success in the Open, one man stands tall over all others in the modern era, and he is Thomas Sturges Watson, better known simply as Tom Watson. A long time personal favourite golfer of mine, this chapter relates the story of Tom's fifth Open victory at Royal Birkdale in 1983, an event which I was privileged to enjoy first hand, having been lucky enough to land the dream summer holiday job for the entire week, which meant I would get to see the 112th Open Championship from inside the ropes.

Firstly I would like to go back in time and compare the early influences on Watson's golfing career to Seve Ballesteros. Both players turned professional in the early 1970s, Watson in 1971, and Ballesteros in 1974. Watson was introduced to the game at the age of six by his father, who was a scratch golfer at Kansas City Country Club, Missouri. "Tommy" loved to compete with his father and his older brother Ridge, and this is no doubt where he developed his competitive edge. By the time Watson was thirteen years old, he was outplaying both, and he had the bug. He would play every day from March to September, and apparently spent a lot of time working on his short game, so another trait in common with Ballesteros.

But their two backgrounds were totally different, where as Ballesteros was born into a poor farming family, Watson had a very privileged and structured upbringing, attending school at an all boys prep-school, and being brought up to be the "All American Boy" who was good at a number of sports, including football where he starred as quarterback, basketball and in the summer, golf.

Watson was earmarked for one of America's top universities, Stanford, where he graduated in psychology in 1971, but wasn't sure what he wanted to do, and like many of his friends at college he spent a lot of his time thinking about joining up for the Vietnam War. The story goes that he had an epiphany whilst playing on his own one evening under the stars on Stanford Golf Course, when he asked himself why he was out there, and what was it that he did best, and Tom decided there and then that golf was his future, and it was time to turn professional.

Watson had won four Missouri State Championships in five years from 1967 to 1971, so the winning pedigree was already there, and his first Major impact would come in the 1974 US Open at Winged Foot when he led after three rounds, but then fell away in the final round allowing Hale Irwin to win. Despite this disappointment, the great Byron Nelson now took a close personal interest in his career, becoming both a friend and mentor, developing Watson's mindset as well as grooving his swing. Even to this day, Watson's swing appears as effective, repeatable and rhythmically beautiful as it did back then, which is no doubt why his star has shone so brightly for so long on the golf course.

If the US Open would be Watson's ultimate goal, he rather surprised himself by winning the Open Championship at Carnoustie in 1975 at the first time of asking. Only four other golfers, Jock Hutchinson (1921), Ben Hogan (1953), Tony Lema (1964), and Ben Curtis (2003) have won the Open on debut,.... and Watson openly admits to not liking links golf at this stage of his career, and struggling with the demands of it, the unusual bounces, the blind shots, which were alien to most American courses. His conversion to links golf was therefore a gradual process, as he learnt to feel his way rather than power his way round.

Watson's golfing career, his reputation and his standing in the game were all enhanced by the great rivalry he enjoyed with Jack Nicklaus. On a number of occasions they would go head to head in the final round of a major tournament, including the 1977 US Masters, which saw Watson narrowly win his first Green Jacket, and most notably at the Open Championship at Turnberry in the same year. Nicklaus and Watson matched each other on the first two days with rounds of 68 and 70, and paired together over the last two rounds, they both shot stunning 65s to be tied for the lead three shots clear of the chasing pack. Playing together again in the final round, the two matched each other shot for shot, striding parched fairways, like gun slingers, in what would be affectionately known as "the Duel in the Sun".

Nicklaus was two shots ahead as they stood on the 13th tee, but three back nine birdies from Watson, and a short missed birdie putt by Nicklaus on the 17th put him one shot ahead playing the last. Watson drilled a beauty down the middle, but Nicklaus, pressing for extra length pushed his drive into heavy rough. Watson then hit the perfect seven iron to less than three feet, and surely it was game over, but against all the odds Nicklaus hacked his second onto the front of the green, and then measured every angle of what was about a 30 foot putt, which of course found the middle of the hole for an unlikely birdie.

Nicklaus had at least made his opponent win it. However, Watson was up to the challenge, calmly holing his short putt, for a second successive round of 65, to claim his second Open title, the pair embracing each other in a moment of mutual respect, Watson in a bright green shirt, Nicklaus in customary bright yellow, such were the golfing fashions of the day! How I wish I had been there, but to get a feel for how big a moment this was, have a listen to Andrew Proud's recollections on YouTube, which perfectly describe the true essence of being there.

The third placed golfer was Hubert Green, who finished 10 shots behind Nicklaus, and 11 behind Watson. There is no better sight than seeing two great sportsman at the height of their powers, competing in the right way, and after everything, Watson and Nicklaus left the 18th green, arms around each other, as only great champions can.

More recently, the Open did produce another equally thrilling climax in 2016, when Swede Henrik Stenson edged out the 2013 Open Champion, Phil Mickelson, at Royal Troon. At least on a par with Watson and Nicklaus' best efforts, the sustained quality of golf by both players over the closing 36 holes was sensational, Stenson shooting a final round of 63 to Mickelson's 65, to win by three shots, with third placed JB Holmes a distant 14 shots behind.

Watson had an outstanding year in 1980, collecting a third Open Championship in Scotland, this time at Muirfield Golf Club, thanks largely to a brilliant third round of 64, winning by four shots from Lee Trevino. A second Masters title followed in 1981, but it was the US Open that Watson most wanted to win, and in 1982 the venue was very much to Watson's liking, Pebble Beach, the only regular links course on the US Open rota. Watson was able to realise his dream because of a brilliant if unlikely chip in for a birdie two on the 17th hole, which once again saw him overtake Jack Nicklaus to the title.

But Tom Watson wasn't done just yet, and the following month he was able to carry his good form across the Atlantic to Royal Troon, where he edged past fellow American Bobby Clampett and Zimbabwean Nick Price to claim his fourth Open Championship, by a single shot. Watson had now won the Open on four different Scottish courses, Carnoustie, Turnberry, Muirfield and Troon, and his victory at Troon meant that he also became only the third golfer in the post-war period after Hogan in 1953, and Trevino in 1971, to win the US Open and the Open in the same year. (Tiger Woods also achieved this in 2000)

So the scene was set for the 1983 Open Championship played at Royal Birkdale Golf Club in July 1983, the venue which had previously crowned four great champions: Peter Thomson, (1954 and 1965), Arnold Palmer (1961), Lee Trevino (1971) and Jonny Miller (1976). Undoubtedly Tom Watson went into the tournament as favourite, but as always there were plenty of contenders, and this would prove to be a very special week for me too, because thanks to a very good school friend whose Dad just happened to be on the Championship organising committee, I had the privilege of a free pass to every day, as well as a paid job for the entire week which included the four practice days and the four days of competition.

Not all the players arrive at the Open venue at the same time. Some like to arrive early to ensure they have ample time to practise, others who may already know the course well tend to leave it later. The first official day of practice, Sunday 10th July, was therefore fairly quiet, and reporting for duty, Rob and I found out that we were working together on the Practice Round Starter Board for the first four days, which basically meant it was our job to approach the players directly and ask them who they were playing with, and what tee-off time they would like to book. We then placed this information on the board for spectators to see. We were required to be at the club no later than 7am every day, and we got busier day by day.

From about 8.30am there was always quite a throng of spectators lingering around the board, which was positioned close to the professional's shop, the players' locker room and the practice putting green. Rob and I had been entrusted with the door entry code to the player's locker room. Widely regarded as a final sanctuary for the players, a place for quiet contemplation and focus, away from the prying eyes of the press and general public, we quickly realised that so long as we were on our best behaviour, this would both be the best place to get the information we required, and also a great way to meet our heroes in the flesh.

On the Monday practice day, it must have been my turn to go to the locker room, and who should I all but bump into but none other than Jack Nicklaus himself! "Good morning sir" I managed to squeak out, "who will you be playing with today please?" Jack Nicklaus looked at me and said "Sonny, put me down with Player, Weiskopf and Trevino today for 9.30am". As the diary says, all the big men were out, Jack, Tom, Lanny, Seve, Ben and Hale. There were some pretty big four balls going out and it was quite a thrill to put up the names one by one and listen to people's reactions as you did so.

And perhaps the best part of this job was that once the players were out on the course, you got to follow them too, to walk the fairways, and hear all their banter at close quarters, and in Trevino's case he just never shut up. I followed this spectacular four ball from the 10th-14th, and watched them all play out each hole, and then practise their putting and bunker shots from all sides. Gary Player, well regarded as one of the finest bunker players of all time, also gave those lucky enough to be in ear shot a lesson on bunker play, including how to play a plugged ball, and then he would play the actual shot to demonstrate.

On the Wednesday, final practice day, the players were getting much more serious in their approach, squeezing in a final round or nine holes, and generally spending more time on the range and the putting greens with their caddies and coaches, honing their games for the first round proper. I remember being allowed into the Main Clubhouse at lunchtime to witness a special presentation to Arnold Palmer, who had won back in 1961, and played a miracle recovery shot from some "blackberry bushes" on the 16th in the final round to secure his first Open. Although Palmer was now in the twilight of his competitive career at 53 years old, he battled through to make the cut right on the mark, and then produced a fine 68 in the third round to please his many fans.

The craic in Open Week was just amazing, and we were out every night on the town, and there was no shortage of good hostelries in Southport to sample, though it would appear that one pub, "The Fish", was visited every single night for eight consecutive nights. Everyone who can get back to Southport, does get back for Open Week, and so there was a great crowd of young people for me to meet, and we had an absolute ball all week. One of Rob's mates was called Dennis, and he shared a christian name with one of the local golfers who had qualified for the Open, called Dennis Durnian. Durnian would finish in a tie for eighth place, and in the second round produced an Open record for the lowest nine-hole total, with a remarkable outward 28. To this day, Rob's mate Dennis is still called "Front Nine".

Work on the four days of competition was different. Rob got the top job, which was whizzing to and from the practice ground ferrying golfers on a golf cart, whilst I had a variety of jobs which included working with the gentleman who was in charge of the leaderboards, both the giant board in the centre of the course, but also all the individual greenside boards, which were all hooked up to central control by walkie-talkie, so that every score for every player could be relayed back to the mainboard as it happened. He would hand me the keys to his automatic car and ask me to go and buy some lunch for him, and also to pick up a pack of beers.

I was also in charge of litter collection for one part of the course, which meant handing out plastic bin liners to children from one of the local schools, and meeting up with them every two hours, to gather the rubbish in one place, and then hand out more bin liners. In between all this, I made my way to and from the 4th, the first of Birkdale's short holes, where my friends from Nottingham University, were working, co-ordinating all the players' scores back to main control from the greenside tower. This was also a very advantageous viewing spot to see the players hit their long irons to the green from the raised tee.

There were some memorable moments to report during the tournament. Firstly, and on a totally unexpected and frustrating note, the Championship committee was suddenly faced with a very serious act of vandalism which was perpetrated in the early hours of the third morning of competition when supporters of a convicted killer called Dennis Kelly cut slogans into the turf of the 6th green. The vandalism was only spotted by the greenkeepers at first light, and the only action possible was to ask the players to lift and place on the putting surface for the rest of the tournament.

And there were a number of shots that I particularly remember. The first may have been in the second round, and I was taking time out to follow Jack Nicklaus for a few holes, and on the relatively short and easy par four 5th hole, Jack played his second shot from the right hand rough, and got a flier. There quickly followed shouts of fore, as the ball hit the TV tower stanchion at the back of the green on the full not far from where I was standing, only for the ball to ricochet neatly back onto the green about 20 foot from the pin. If the TV tower had not been there, his ball would have ended up on the side of a grassy dune some 50 yards through the green, and the ricochet could of course have gone anywhere. Even the best players can make serious misjudgements, and luck always plays its part in sport, at any level.

Craig Stadler, who had won the 1982 Masters, was fastest

out of the blocks. The American, also known as the Walrus because of his portly build and big moustache, was the first round leader with a stunning 64, a lead he would hold after two rounds on eight under par. Close on his heels and one shot behind were the ever present Tom Watson (67, 68) and the motormouthed Mexican, Lee Trevino (69, 66). England's Nick Faldo was a shot further back after consecutive rounds of 68, with Hale Irwin nicely placed one shot further back on five under par. Watson swapped positions at the end of the third round with Stadler and ominously for the rest of the field now led the tournament for the first time by one stroke, with Faldo a shot further back, Trevino still there, and Irwin and another American Andy Bean both within touching distance.

Then there was Hale Irwin's fresh air shot, or as the Americans call it a "whiff", in the third round on the par three 14th hole which I always remember, because I saw it happen. It's the last of the four short holes at Birkdale, all of them, in different ways, wonderful holes. Irwin had hit a great long iron into the heart of the green to 20 feet below the hole, leaving him an outside chance for birdie. Although he hit a good putt which was right on line, frustratingly it came up six inches short, leaving the simplest of tap ins for a safe par three.

What happened next? Don't worry, this isn't "A Question of Sport", but it's probably best to let Hale Irwin himself explain things. "Went up to backhand a six-incher, missed it, finished second to Watson by one stroke. Careless." That's one way to describe it, but it certainly sounded like he was hoping the interviewer would quickly move on and ask another question. It's probably something we have all done, through a momentary lack of concentration, or out of frustration, and on most occasions it doesn't matter too much, but this was the Open Championship, an event Hale Irwin was destined never to win.

So all was set for a very exciting final round, and having organized my litter duties, I headed for the 4th green to watch the later starters come through, and I had a perfect view of a fresh faced Nick Faldo, on the charge, and the third shot of note I recall is his 20 foot birdie putt which unerringly found the centre of the cup, to tumultuous applause. At one stage he would find his name at the top of the leaderboard, and the prospect of a first English born winner since Tony Jacklin in 1969 was suddenly a possibility. Sadly Faldo's charge would fizzle out on the back nine, and he would finish with a 73 for a share of eighth place, but as we know, he would go on to remodel his swing, and win three of his own Open Championships.

The leaderboards were creaking in an attempt to keep up with the last round scoring, and another man on the charge was Australian Graham Marsh, elder brother of Australian cricketer Rod Marsh. He would shoot the best round of the day, an impressive 64, thereby posting an early and very competitive target of seven under par. At one stage Lee Trevino looked like he would also make a back nine charge as he rifled in a trademark eagle at the 13th, but he would run out of steam over the closing holes and finish with a round of 70 for a six under par total.

Which meant only one of three Americans, Hale Irwin,

Andy Bean or Tom Watson could now overhaul Graham Marsh's target, and playing together, both Irwin and Bean would birdie the 17th, and par the 18th to finish tied on eight under par, both posting classy final round 67s. Watson had not enjoyed the best of front nines, but got himself back to the top of the leaderboard by making three birdies on the back nine at the 11th, 13th and crucially at the 16th, where he holed from 15 feet. However he could only manage a par five at the 17th, so he now stood on the 18th tee, knowing that all he needed was a par to win the Open.

The 18th at Royal Birkdale is an awesome finishing hole, and plays 473 yards long off the championship tee. The tee is perched high on a dune, and you are faced with an intimidating drive, with a long carry to the fairway, and there is out of bounds all the way down the right side. The hole plays as a dog leg right from this tee, and if played into the wind, as on July 17th 1983, even the professionals were close to their limits in terms of reaching the green in two shots. The green is well bunkered on both sides, and is situated directly in front of the outstandingly impressive bright white painted art deco clubhouse, which is capped by an iconic clock tower. It is a fine finishing hole, worthy of deciding any major championship.

If you watch the TV highlights just after Watson had unleashed his second shot, you will note that the 18th fairway was bedlam, as those spectators who had been lined up behind Watson, almost encroaching in his swing arc, or so it seemed, were now running as fast as they could to get the best vantage point as close to the green as the marshalls would allow. There were literally hundreds of people, and as it was back then, the players, and their caddies had to fight their way forward through the crowds to get to the green. But I was lucky enough to have a pass for one of the greenside stands, which meant that I could see back down the fairway, and track Watson's ball all the way onto the green.

This is definitely the best shot I have seen by a golfer in a pressure situation, and even having hit a very good drive, Watson still had 213 yards into the wind for his second shot, and needed a career two iron to get home. Taking little time, Watson addressed his ball, gave a customary Watson waggle, and then swung sweetly and nipped the ball off the turf, striking the ball low and beneath the wind. The galleries engulfed him before the ball had landed, but judging from our cheers, he must have known it was both on line, and on the green. In Watson's own words delivered in his attractive American tone... "I busted that two-iron as well as I could hit it". The trajectory was true, the line dead on the flag, and the ball came up 15 foot short, and as Peter Alliss remarked "those are the shots that champions are made of", adding when Watson lagged his first putt, "what did old Harry Vardon say, when you've got two for it, take 'em".

In the space of just nine years, Watson now had his fifth Open title, and had drawn level with those legends of the game, Braid, Taylor and Thompson, and with Watson at the peak of his game and still only 33 years old, it seemed then that it was just a matter of time that Harry Vardon's record of six Open victories would be matched by him. The very next year, Watson would also have the chance of completing the full set of Open wins in Scotland at the very home of golf, St Andrews.

The 1984 Open at St Andrews would prove just as exciting, with four players in the hunt at the start of the final round, Bernhard Langer and Seve Ballesteros for Europe playing in the penultimate group, 2 shots behind the joint leaders, Australian Ian Baker-Finch, and after a supreme third round of 66, five times champion, none other than Tom Watson. Ballesteros and Watson were tied after 16 holes on 11 under par, and whilst Watson over shot the green at the infamous 17th Road Hole to make bogey, Ballesteros was fist pumping his birdie on the 18th to secure his third Open.

Watson's run for a third consecutive Open title had come up just short, and perhaps somewhat surprisingly, his Birkdale triumph would prove to be his eighth and final major championship victory. He came close again at Troon in 1989 when Mark Calcavecchia won in a three way play-off, and although Watson's swing looked as fluid and repeatable as it ever had done, and whilst he remained fit and competitive, and practised as hard as he always did, gradually his putting stroke lost its surety, particularly at short range.

As soon as Watson reached 50 years old he took the Senior Tour by storm, winning a further six major titles including three Senior Open championships, at three Scottish courses, Turnberry in 2003, Royal Aberdeen in 2005, and Muirfield in 2007. A gradual convert, Tom Watson quickly fell in love with Links Golf, particularly in Scotland, and remains a passionate supporter of it. A traditionalist, his perfect day out would I think be a round of golf at one of his favourite courses, Royal Dornoch, where he is now one of a very few Honorary Members. And it would be remiss of me not to end this Tom Watson chapter without recounting the 2009 Open Championship.

The 2009 Open was held at one of Tom's favourite courses, where he had already won in 1977, and again in 2003. At 59 years old, the competitive juices were still flowing and a return to Turnberry and the Ailsa Course where he was so at home was surely going to be a perfect way to bow out from the championship. And when calm and sunny conditions greeted the players on the first day, Watson rolled back the years with an opening bogey free round of 65.

High winds and showers on day two provided the players with a reality check, but Watson recovered from a slow start to finish strongly, helped by long birdie putts at the 16th and 18th to tie the lead at five under. In the third round, and in similar conditions, he shot a one over par 71 to take a one shot lead into the final round. Surely Watson would be caught, after all it was 26 years since his last win at Royal Birkdale, and also he was nearly 60 years old. But if he could win, what a fairy tale ending this would be for gentleman Tom Watson who had given so much to the Open over the years.

Two Englishmen looked like they might be the ones to spoil Tom's party, firstly Chris Wood who finished early and posted one under par despite a bogey at the last when his second shot ran through the back of the green, and then Lee Westwood who had worked his way into the lead, and looked odds on to break his major duck, only for a clumsy finish which saw him bogey three of the last four holes, including a costly three putt at the last hole, to tie with Wood at one under par.

American Stewart Cink had quietly gone about his business all day, and went under the radar until late in his round, and when he suddenly holed a 15 foot birdie putt at the last to move to two under par, he became the leader in the clubhouse. No sooner had Cink holed his putt, remarkably Tom Watson birdied the par five 17th hole, to claim the outright lead again at three under par, and suddenly the greatest story in the history of the Open Championship was about to come true.

Shades of Birkdale 1983, as Watson stood on the 18th tee, all he needed was a par four at the last to win his sixth Open title, and tie Vardon's record. I can only imagine the nerves he must have felt, but you wouldn't have known it, as he hit a fairway splitting drive, leaving a straight forward eight iron approach. Thoughts must have gone back to 1977 and his duel in the sun with Nicklaus when he hit the perfect approach, and so he did once again, nipping his eight iron perfectly to land in the middle of the green, but just as Cink's ball had checked to settle hole high, Watson's ball ran on and just through the back of the green.

Watson opted to use his putter from off the green, but was too firm, and he ran it by the hole leaving him what was probably a 10 foot putt for par. Perhaps the gravity of the moment finally took its toll, and a tentative putt followed, and the moment had passed, as Stuart Cink went on to win the four hole play off with anticlimactic ease.

Watson had come within a whisker of creating history, but perhaps that is the beauty of links golf, an extra gust of wind, or a hard bounce, those can be the margins, as Tom Watson would appreciate more than most. The bogey at the last was a bitter pill for Tom to swallow, and at the time there was probably only one person in golf who would not have wished for a different outcome.

Watson's Open career had opened with a birdie at the 18th at Carnoustie in 1975 to earn a place in the play-off against Jack Newton, and in 2009, it was Stewart Cink who did the same to Watson at Turnberry. Tom Watson's farewell Open would fittingly be at St Andrews in 2015, and he said "This place is special, it will always be the golf course people think about when they think of links golf… it has been a great run since 1975 when I first played across the links of Carnoustie."

On a personal note, my week at Royal Birkdale had been an amazing adventure, and it also earned me £94, which was quite a lot of money in those days! It was an absolute privilege to be at such a prestigious event all week, and I am so grateful to have had such an opportunity.

I made lots of life-long friends that week, and would over the next few years travel over to Southport from Yorkshire for parties which typically ran well into the night, but whatever the hour, we always got up early for an 8am Sunday morning fourball.

It was also a tradition to play the 18th hole off the championship tee, which for golfers of my standard simply made a tough hole a lot harder! There was no way I could reach the green in two shots, but the dream of matching Watson and making your very own par at the last was enough to raise hopes. On one memorable occasion, I was partnered with Rob, and the match was poised all square down the last. An average drive just made the fairway, but then a topped second shot left me a full three wood into the green, and my claim to fame is hitting a career best wood into the heart of the green, and then holing my twelve foot putt for a par four (net three) to win the hole and the match. You should have heard the crowds cheer!

Chapter 6
Escape to Victory

23rd March 1985: Bradford City 5 Brentford 4

My father started taking me to Valley Parade when I was 12 years old, and I recall a very inauspicious first match on Boxing Day 1975, a game of very few chances, and totally unremarkable in every way, which rightly ended Bradford City 0, Scunthorpe United 0. However, my first steps had been taken, and Division 4 football did not appear to have put me off, and over the next 10 years Dad and I would be regular attendees watching City from the Midland Road stand. We usually found a spot near half-way, and Dad would always ask someone to clear a space for me so I could get to the front, and get a clear pitch-side view. We got to know the fans around us, and one particular old fellow always made me laugh, as he would repeat the words "half-way line" over and over again, every match, in a strange screechy sort of accent, and always when City were taking a goal-kick. I never understood what he meant, and still don't!

How many fathers take their sons to watch their local football team? Hundreds, thousands, all over the country, and in some cases grandfathers, daughters, wives, the whole family... this is very much the essence of football, and a bond is forged over time between fans, players and their club, and it happens all over the world. So this chapter sets out to describe two events which for me encapsulated Bradford City's most successful season for decades, one breathless match against Brentford played on the 23rd March 1985, and one day of celebration on May 11th 1985 which ended in tragedy for so many families.

But first, please indulge me, as I try and set the scene in the lead up to the 1984/85 season. My early City heroes from the mid 70s onwards were Cyril Casey Marcel Podd, better known just as "Ces", Terry Dolan, Joe Cooke and Don Hutchins, and I also liked the fact that Terry Dolan never missed a penalty kick either! As well as getting down to Valley Parade, Dad and I would also try and take in the odd away match too at Halifax Town, and in 1978, I remember 4th Division Bradford City being drawn in the League Cup against 2nd Division Burnley, and pulling off a worthy 1-1 draw against the Clarets at what I recall being a huge and impressive ground (Turf Moor), thanks to a Don Hutchins goal. I also recall we lost the replay the following week having been 2-0 up at half time. Steve Kindon and Brian Noble were in the Burnley team at that time.

City's fortunes changed for the better when Roy McFarland came to manage at the start of the 1981/2 season, which led to a second place finish and promotion to Division 3, and although McFarland was poached back to Derby County at the start of the following season, the new management team comprising two stalwarts of Don Revie's great Leeds United team, Trevor Cherry and his assistant Terry Yorath took charge and steadied the ship.

The following summer – 1983 – City's financial position was so serious that they were forced into receivership. They were rescued by former Chairman Stafford Heginbotham and Jack Tordoff which marked the start of a successful era for the club.

The 1984/85 Bradford City squad was small in terms of numbers, and especially by today's standards, but it did possess an excellent balance of youth and experience. Bobby Campbell had been City's top scorer on three previous occasions, but had been sold out of necessity to Derby County to ensure the club survived. After an unhappy few months at the Baseball Ground, City re-signed him and he combined well with co-striker John Hawley in the second half of the 1983/84 season which saw City finish strongly in a creditable seventh position.

At the other end of the pitch, Eric McManus was starting his third season as goalkeeper at Valley Parade, and had bags of second division experience from his early days at Notts County, as did recently signed Chris Withe from Newcastle United, and as did central defender Dave Evans, formerly at Aston Villa, and signed on a free transfer by Cherry from Halifax Town. Still only 24 years old Peter Jackson had been at City for seven years, and he and Evans would quickly form a strong partnership at the heart of the Bantams' defence. Adding into the mix the undoubted experience of Trevor Cherry and Terry Yorath when needed, this team possessed plenty of know-how.

Cherry was also indebted to the Coventry connection, signing three players who had all started their careers and played together in the Coventry City youth team. Firstly, there was utility player Greg Abbott who had been given a free transfer in 1982; secondly right winger John Hendrie was let go at the end of the 1984 season; and thirdly the City squad was to be reinforced by the signing of another Coventry player, midfielder Martin Singleton, in January 1985. Still only 20 years old, Stuart McCall was now a burgeoning talent in the centre of midfield, and Mark Ellis at 22 years old was also a regular in the team, and an exciting presence on the left wing. At 19 years old, Don Goodman was another fine young talent who would play his part through the season.

Although City lost three of their first four away games of the season, their home form was excellent, and they put together a 13 match unbeaten streak just before Christmas to stake their claim as title contenders, and the fans were getting used to winning, and were enjoying Bobby Campbell's run of good form in front of goal too, and by the middle of February after important back to back 2-0 wins against promotion hopefuls Bristol Rovers at home and Hull City away, City had opened up a 10 point lead at the top of the table.

Miserly in defence, and increasingly potent up front, City were flying high, the players were clearly enjoying their football, and the fans, whilst not complacent, were convinced that promotion was theirs. John Hendrie, after an unhappy period at Coventry City, remembers his first season at the Valley with great fondness, describing the team as a very tight unit, on and off the pitch, with a family feel to it.

Trevor Cherry and Terry Yorath had done a great job in building the right atmosphere for the players to express themselves, which also included encouraging the team to socialise together as much as possible. Bobby Campbell was a legend in his own lunchtime it would appear, often saying after training that he was going to church, which everyone knew meant he was partaking of the insalubrious delights on offer at the Belle Vue Hotel, and then taking it upon himself to protect the younger players on match days....Hendrie describes Bobby as everybody's minder, and that he had "more sets of teeth in his elbow than anyone else in the history of the game".

Stafford Heginbotham was also quite a character. He liked to be part of the action and on match days, home or away, it was customary for him to pop his head round the changing room door at about 2.50pm, and say "a little bonus lads, £200 on me if we win today". The next game he would come in and say the same thing, except offer double or quits, and Hendrie remembers with a chuckle that as they kept winning, the amount rose higher every week, and ran well into four figures. Of course they never ever saw a bean of it, rather the boss would sanction an end of season trip to Magaluf by way of a thank you. Heginbotham was also the proud wearer of a wig, and sported either his summer or his winter wig, which was a constant source of amusement for everyone in the dressing room.

It was these close team ties that would soon be put to the

ultimate test, and the first of these tests came on Saturday 23rd March when City entertained Brentford who were in the bottom half of the table. On paper, this should have been a comfortable home victory, and with a quarter of the season still to play, this was not the day to slip up and allow the chasing pack an unexpected opportunity to make up ground.

There were just over 6,000 fans at the ground that day, not City's biggest crowd of the season, but bigger than normal, and I recall there being a quiet confidence and expectation amongst the supporters. However, such positive thoughts were very quickly cast aside as Frank McLintock's Brentford had the effrontery to not only take the lead, but to score three times in the first 20 minutes of the game. City were 3-0 down at home, and the crowds' good humour had quickly turned to stunned silence, but call it blind optimism, I never once lost faith, and always thought that we would fight back to win the game.

But if City were to win this game, they needed to get their skates on, and play the sort of eye catching attacking football that they had been playing for most of the season. What followed next was certainly one of the most exciting matches I have ever witnessed, and must rate as one of the best comebacks ever (perhaps only surpassed by City's recent 4-2 FA Cup victory at Stamford Bridge in January 2015). Perhaps not surprisingly in a 2012 poll of Bradford City fans they rated this match at No 11 in the list of City's all time greatest matches.

City soon started to display their fighting spirit, raising the tempo of their game, and gradually they began to dominate play. In football pressure nearly always results in a goal, and it came as no surprise to anyone when City pulled one back through a low shot from Hendrie, and he repeated the formula on 32 minutes to get City right back in it. There was an extraordinary flurry of incidents just before half-time, when both sides had the ball in the net, only for both to be ruled out for offside, and Hendrie could have scored his hat trick as he ran all of 40 yards to be one on one with the keeper, only to shoot wide.

According to Hendrie, half-time bollockings were something to avoid. The management had these off to a tee, and where as Trevor Cherry would be more measured and play the "Good Cop" role, Terry Yorath would pile in and turn the air blue and play his part as the "Bad Cop". It was good teamwork, but on this occasion, and because City had got themselves back in the game, this half-time talk was very positive, and it must have hit the mark because within 15 seconds of the restart Mark Ellis had put City level after a great move down the left, a cross from Withe, a nod down from Campbell, and a fine strike from 15 yards.

However Brentford had not read the script very thoroughly, and were far from done. Their striker Robbie Cooke scored his third goal of the match to put the visitors back in front after 53 minutes, and once again City had to dig deep. It had been a frenetic end to end game up to this point, but for the home fans suddenly and for the first time in the match, and as time ticked away, it looked like defeat was a possibility. More City pressure paid off, following another cross from Withe, which led to a fortuitous own goal and

City were back on level terms.

John Hawley came on as substitute for Don Goodman, and following a Chris Withe corner which was nodded on by Dave Evans, there was Hawley, ever the classy finisher, in the right place at the right time to fire home from four yards out with a powerful rising shot on 76 minutes. What an impact he had made, but there was still 14 minutes to play plus whatever stoppage time there might be.

At that point no one in the ground knew how this game would finish and to be honest I don't recall much of what happened in this final period, but I suspect it was pretty nervy stuff, with chances at either end. I suppose when you think how many goals get scored in the last 10 minutes of matches, remarkably that was the end of the scoring. Not that anyone in Bradford City colours was bemoaning the final score line, and I suppose having already witnessed nine goals, spectators and players were all ready for a breather.

Final Score: Bradford City 5 Brentford 4.

An absolute humdinger of a game that had just about everything, action packed from start to finish, swings of momentum, nine goals, and if you were a City supporter, another important three points. Trevor Cherry, ever the defender, described his team's defending as slack, and the worst performance of the season, but also said that City always looked like scoring, and went on to praise the amazing character of his young team.

My own overriding feeling was an even stronger sense of belief that this was going to be our year, and that we would now go on to win the league. For even when the chips had been really down, I had thought the game could still be won, and the players had proved me right. After all, if you can come back from 3-0 down, you can come back from just about anything.

Chapter 7
Phoenix from the Ashes

11th May 1985: Bradford City 0 Lincoln City 0 – match abandoned

City's thrilling victory against Brentford was an important stepping stone on the way to being crowned Division 3 Champions, as it was the catalyst for an unbeaten 10 game streak, and but for back to back defeats to Bournemouth and then Reading at home, the title would have been secured well before City's visit to Burnden Park for the penultimate match of the season against Bolton on May 6th. Early goals from Stuart McCall and Bobby Campbell settled any nerves and led to a 2-0 victory, and City knew then that they were Champions, and the party could now begin.

City had last been in Division 2 in 1937, and the wait was now finally over, and as luck would have it, the celebrations could take place in front of their own fans, just a few days later, on Saturday 11th May, in the final match of the season against Lincoln City.

Dad and I were not going to miss the final match of the

season for any money, and we headed off nice and early in good spirits, and very much looking forward to being part of the celebrations. We parked in our usual position on Canal Road, and walked up with lots of other happy fans, and got our usual half-way line spot in the Midland Road stand in good time, having splashed out 50p for the Official Souvenir Programme which was emblazoned with the words:

"Division 3 Champions" 1984-1985.

The programme congratulated City on their outstanding landmark achievement, and it also included thank yous to some of the season's key players.... "What a season for Stuart", who it said had turned down lucrative offers from Newcastle and Chelsea to stay at City next season, and it also highlighted "The Debt to Bobby Campbell" who broke the club's all time goal scoring record during the season. Dave Evans and skipper Peter Jackson, along with Hendrie, Abbott and Singleton, the latter forming the Coventry connection, were all mentioned in despatches too.

The Trevor Cherry Column was suitably upbeat too and I quote:

We've had an excellent season and I'd like to think the team have provided good entertainment for everyone... I would also like to thank everyone who has supported us this season, and hopefully it will be an enjoyable afternoon today, whatever the result. I hope you have a good summer and all get behind us next season. We've had tremendous support this season, and when you consider that we have been taking more than 3,000 supporters to some recent away games, that is a very high proportion of our home crowd... Obviously I am delighted we won the Third Division championship. We've got a very determined bunch of players who want to win things, and they have given of their best all season, which is pleasing for a manager.

We were also told that there would be presentations before the match, and that in the crowd that day, there were delegates from the city's twin towns, who had been in Bradford for the 40th anniversary of VE Day on the 8th May. And we were all invited to cheer on the team at the civic reception at City Hall the following afternoon, or line the streets for the open topped bus parade which would leave from Valley Parade bound for City Hall.

The presentations did indeed take place before the match started, which in itself was quite unusual, and The 3rd Division Trophy was presented to captain Peter Jackson, and all the players received their medals. And in a touching thank you from the players, all 12 of them lined up on the half way line holding aloft a board, each board spelling out on either side the same message "THANK YOU FANS". The celebrations over, the players could now concentrate on the game, which to be honest after all that excitement was a bit of an anti-climax, and quite pedestrian.

If my other chapters in this book have concentrated on match winning performances, and individual moments of sporting brilliance, if truth be told I have no recollection of what occurred in the first half. The reality was that this was a game that had nothing riding on it, as City were already crowned Champions, and Lincoln were clear of relegation. John Hendrie recalls that the other mitigating factor in the first half was the strength of the wind, which Bradford had chosen to play into, which was not helping the home team play their usual brand of attractive football, but would as we will see play a significant part in what was to follow soon afterwards.

There have been many accounts of what happened just before half-time, and in the fullness of time which is now 35 years, my recollections may only be partly accurate, and possibly out of sequence, but they do appear to be largely backed up by subsequent explanations. I remember pointing out to Dad that I could see a flame in the stand opposite, and although the ground was all but full, I recall there being a number of empty spaces in the Main Stand in what I later understood to be G Block, which was the end of the Main Stand nearest to the Kop End.

How did the fire start? The official explanation which certainly seems the most likely, describes it as an accident, and probably it was started by a discarded cigarette or match, which may then have set light to a plastic cup. I don't recall how long the initial flame was alight and visible for, but I would guess about a minute or so, and there appeared to be three people sitting where the flame was and from a distance it did look like a plastic cup was alight. It is assumed that whatever was alight fell down between the stair gaps and under the old wooden stand, where it ignited the dry rubbish which had gathered over previous years. Ironically, the old wooden stand which our family timber business had supplied the wood for at the start of the century was due to be pulled down and replaced with a concrete stand for the start of the 1985/6 season.

The game continued for another couple of minutes or so, but increasingly there appeared to be movement amongst the spectators in the Main Stand, which may also have had something to do with half-time approaching, and perhaps the police had already started moving spectators away from the location of the fire. Did I see a policeman called to the incident, and did he try to cover or put out the flame with his helmet... this bit I can't be sure about, but the thought still lingers in my mind even after all these years.

Then everything appeared to happen very quickly and just as the match was stopped by the referee, and the players were led off the field, spectators began to spill out onto the pitch from the Main Stand, as the flames, fanned by the strong winds, took hold with alarming speed and engulfed first that end of the stand in the area of G Block, and then very quickly the entire length of the highly combustible bitumen and felt clad roof of the stand.

Yorkshire Television was covering the big game, and had erected a camera tower directly above where we were standing on top of the Midland Road stand where commentator John Helm was positioned, and from where he would bravely describe unfolding events, pictures and words soon finding their way to the wider audience of ITV's World of Sport. Directly below him, we, like everyone else around us were just stunned at what was happening in front of us, and even at a distance of 60 yards across the pitch, such was the ferocity of the fire, I recall it was very difficult to face it for any length of time, and having to look away from it on a number of occasions.

In what appeared to be a very short space of time, and experts were later to confirm that it had only taken four and a half minutes for the whole stand to go up in flames, there were quickly hundreds of people on the pitch. To be honest, it was very confusing and difficult to see at ground level exactly what was happening, and whilst we did see people jumping over the wall of the Main Stand, and one person's hair was alight, we had no appreciation at the time just how serious this all was.

We were held in the ground for at least another 20 minutes, before being asked to leave, which we did in a very orderly and subdued manner via the stairwell exit in the corner of the ground between Midland Road and Holywell Ash Lane. I then clearly recall coming out onto Midland Road, and as we started walking back towards Canal Road, we encountered a line of perhaps 10 policemen, all of whom were slumped against the wall by the turnstiles, all looking exhausted with smoke stained faces, and it was only then that the severity of the incident started to dawn. Even then, and in common with many others, there was no understanding that there had been any fatalities, something that was backed up by Telegraph and Argus Sports reporter, David Markham, who had been directly opposite us, at the back of the Main Stand covering the match in the press box.

To his left, he could see that there were police trying to sort out the disturbance, but then he could also see flames, and when the roof caught light, he made the sound decision to leave the press box, and make his way down to the pitch, along with many others, deeming that the pitch was the safest place to be, and in the knowledge that the gates at the back of the stand would be locked. He recalls there being an orderly exodus of fans to the front of the stand, despite seeing the flames leap onto the roof, and hearing the crackling noise of the burning wood. He was also worried about his two teenage sons who were also in the Main Stand, but in different locations, but thankfully all made it to safety.

Not everyone knew the layout of the Main Stand as well as David Markham, and naturally many spectators made for the exits, which were at the top of the stands, close to the turnstiles where they had entered, and it would be here that most of the fatalities took place, in the narrow upper corridor, as many of the exits remained padlocked. The number of fatalities would have been considerably higher had it not been possible to break open some of the gates.

Thick engulfing blinding black smoke was also a factor for these unfortunate fans. Martin Fletcher who lost four members of his immediate family on the day, and writing in his excellent book "56 – The Story of the Bradford Fire" describes the true horror of what happened next, and how he was separated from his family, and how against the odds, he incredibly made it out onto the pitch.

The players were also caught up in the chaos. Initially, they were ushered into the changing rooms, and had thought the cause of the incident might be hooliganism, but were then quickly advised that there was a fire, and were all told to leave the changing rooms immediately and exited the ground through the offices, spilling out onto South Parade and Holywell Ash Lane where, still in their kit, they mingled with fans, black smoke billowing about them, some fans collapsing from the smoke in front of them.

The players also had their families, partners and friends to worry about, and whilst some of the younger players were ushered away to safety, some of the management staff and players like skipper Peter Jackson, Terry Yorath, Dave Evans and John Hawley, stayed out on the pitch, and along with those who had already escaped the burning stand, and along with a number of police officers, all selflessly tried to save others who were now desperately fleeing the stand.

One of the younger players was John Hendrie who was caught up in the chaos, and he remembers being worried for his girlfriend Linda's safety, having no means of contacting her, and he along with other players from both teams, and their families and partners, were ushered away and retreated to the Belle Vue Hotel, on Manningham Lane. Now a well respected television presenter, Gabby Logan, daughter of Terry Yorath, was also there with several members of her family, and recalls how frightening it was as a 12 year old to be in the streets with the enveloping obscuring acrid smoke, and that the cars in the car park were already too hot to touch. They all waited and waited for news, still unsure of the extent of the disaster.

Back in 1985 there were no mobile phones, so we, like

everyone else could not ring home to let the family know of our whereabouts, and we actually took our time getting home, and when we did arrive back in Baildon, we were met by Mum and my younger sister who were both in floods of tears, having seen the harrowing pictures now streaming on ITV's World of Sport, accompanied as they were by John Helm's live, uncensored and upsetting commentary. Of course they had no idea which stand we had been in, and the television images were awful. So many families would go through the same emotions, and for some there would be very sad outcomes.

Thankfully our family was comparatively removed from the real horrors of the day, and for that I am very grateful, though to this day when I think about May 11th 1985, the mind races with questions and what ifs about what might have happened if we had been in a different stand that day, and whether Dad and I would both have made it out safely. In this respect, this tragedy will always be part of me, as it will or was for all the other 11,075 supporters and the players and staff, and emergency workers who were present that day. Having spoken to many who were at the match, each with their own story, I know some are still haunted by the events, racked by "what ifs" and "if onlys", and even a survivor's guilt.

Over the next days, we were to find out the grim facts of the disaster, and learn that a total of 56 fans who had gone to Valley Parade to celebrate their team's achievements that day had very sadly lost their lives, which included 54 City fans, and two Lincoln City Fans. There were also 265 supporters who had been injured, many of whom had serious skin burns, and they had been taken to St Luke's Hospital in Bradford or to Pinderfields Hospital in Wakefield, and these included Stuart McCall's father who needed skin grafts on his hands and head, and Matthew Wildman and his saviour on the day, David Hustler.

City skipper on the day Peter Jackson was interviewed 30 years later about the disaster and commented:

"If you witness something like that you never forget... I had family there and I lost them in the melee, my dad and two brothers. Thank God they all got out alive. What everybody went through that day... was horrendous. It was such a traumatic time. In the days and weeks that followed I was organising fund-raising events and the roster for players to visit Pinderfields and the hospital in Bradford. It was harrowing. When you go to hospital and there's somebody with 40% burns and all they want to talk about is football the following season because we've just been promoted, it was just so humbling".

He went on to say "Nowadays, players would get counselling for what we went through... but as a group, and it was a really young team too, we just got on with it. We just felt we had to do it as a mark of respect for everybody who was there that day. We had to play our part. The fundraising, the hospital visits and the funerals. We just did it. There was no singling anybody out for special mention, we all just got on with it and did it".

And John Hendrie has never forgotten that day either, saying it certainly changed him as a person, and put everything into perspective, and changed his outlook on life. John and Linda were married four weeks later in Coventry, and his footballing career took off, but like many of the players he never forgets, and never misses the annual remembrance ceremony at Centenary Square, because 56 innocent people lost their lives watching a football match. He also remembers how Trevor Cherry, Terry Yorath and Chairman Stafford Heginbotham did their best to try and protect the younger players from the developing trauma and aftermath.

The Bradford Disaster Appeal Fund was set up within 48 hours of the fire, and raised £3.5 million, most of which was distributed to the bereaved families in the same year. The most memorable of hundreds of fundraising events was a reunion on the 1966 World Cup Final starting X1, which began with the original teams of both England and West Germany, and was held at Elland Road in July 1985, a match which England won 6-4. Part of the Appeal funds were raised by "The Crowd", which was a charity supergroup formed specifically to produce a charity record by Gerry Marsden of Gerry and the Pacemakers. The group consisted of singers, actors and TV personalities, and sang "You'll Never Walk Alone" which reached No. 1 on 1st June 1985.

Positives are always difficult to find in these situations, but with the benefit of hindsight, thankfully there were some. Firstly, stadium designers have had to take on board the failings that existed back in 1985, and undoubtedly design and spectator safety particularly in stadia across the UK and round the world has improved significantly. Secondly, and from a medical point of view, and following the great work of the burns units in Bradford and at Pinderfields Hospital, new techniques were developed to deal with these types of horrific injuries.

Thirdly, there were many heroes on that day, ordinary people, all of them ill-equipped to deal with what they saw, but all who disregarded their own safety and helped save lives. And if you wanted to find out more about how the lives of so many people were affected by the disaster, I would recommend you watch the very moving and compassionate documentary produced by BT Sport to coincide with the 35th anniversary of the disaster, which was narrated by Gabby Logan.

Fourthly, and most importantly from a community point of view, and despite so many lives lost, there has been an amazing underlying strength of spirit, togetherness and dignity shown over the years by the bereaved families, the players, the Football Club, its supporters, and the City of Bradford. So that we don't ever forget, there are regular reminders of what happened, both at the ground where 56 seats always remain unoccupied, and where there is a very visible memorial and plaque to commemorate those who died, and another memorial in Centenary Square in the city centre where the annual ceremony takes place.

Supporters of the club, and citizens of the city came together then, and still do, and to illustrate that sometimes there are more important things than football, fans have also taken it upon themselves to stand and applaud in the 56th minute of a key game, as happened in the League Cup

Final at Wembley in 2013 against Swansea. City were already 3-0 down, and their goalkeeper was in the process of being sent off, when the fans showed their appreciation.

To complete a tragic month for football, the Heysel Stadium disaster was to follow less than three weeks later. On the 29th May 1985, and before the start of the European Cup Final between Liverpool and Juventus, trouble broke out on the terraces between rival fans, and 39 fans, mostly Juventus fans, lost their lives crushed against a wall, and a further 600 fans were injured. The Hillsborough disaster would follow on in 1989, when a further 96 fans died watching a football match, this time an FA Cup semi-final between Nottingham Forest and Liverpool.

With other footballing tragedies happening so close to the Bradford City Fire disaster, there is perhaps a feeling amongst Bradfordians that our story whilst not forgotten, has been somewhat overshadowed. However, I believe this has allowed the people of Bradford to deal with the disaster in their own quiet and determined way, which merely goes to demonstrate their collective fortitude and resilience, and desire to rise collectively like a phoenix from the ashes from that awful day.

On a personal note, I left the UK in June 1985 to travel the world for six months, and shortly after my return, my father died from a heart attack. So as fate would have it, May 11th 1985 proved to be the last time Dad and I watched a football match together. I would however like to take this opportunity to thank him for taking me to Valley Parade on so many occasions, in part because of the bonds we forged together, in part because it bonded me to Bradford City. I was also delighted to be able to take my own son to watch City for many of the home games in the 2000 season, and in subsequent seasons, and I remain envious of his being there for the 1-0 "Great Escape" victory in 1999 at the hands of mighty Liverpool.

A professional football club, just like any amateur sports club, will experience highs and lows as their fortunes fluctuate, and Bradford City in my time have certainly known this range of emotion. From the old Division 4 in 1975, to the extreme high and then the depths of tragedy of the 1984/85 season, to attaining Premier League status for two seasons at the turn of the century, to the League Cup Final of 2013, and the FA Cup run of 2015, including perhaps the greatest of all cup shocks against high-flying Chelsea, and now in 2020 we find ourselves playing in the fourth tier of English football again, and Stuart McCall is back at the helm for his third spell as manager.

This is the story of the life of a football club which has gone full circle in the last half-century, which has had to endure more than most, and has still emerged with dignity thanks to the community it represents and which it is an intrinsic part of. This chapter is dedicated to all those who did not return from the match on May 11th 1985.

Chapter 8
I saw Adelaide Alive

November 3rd 1985, Australian Grand Prix

Just one month after the dreadful events at Valley Parade, I had packed my rucksack and set off on a six month round the world trip. The impact of the Bradford fire disaster and the Heysel stadium disaster was felt globally, and at the time I remember how many people immediately associated both events as being part of the same British disease, namely football hooliganism. It certainly was a talking point wherever I went.

Bradford to Adelaide took a few months, as I went via Canada, Hawaii and New Zealand, and I arrived in Sydney on the 24th October, having intercepted some post from an old school friend at Auckland airport, which suggested that the place to be was not the Gold Coast, but Adelaide, because it would be party time as the first ever official Australian Grand Prix was coming to town. Within 24 hours of landing in Australia, I had discovered the questionable sights of Sydney's red light district, Kings Cross, impulsively purchased a one way ticket, and travelled 18 hours or 1,400 kilometres by bus through three different states to join Sarah in Adelaide.

Sarah was living with friends in a suburb of Adelaide called Tranmere, and it can best be described as a mad-house of five similarly aged Aussies who didn't seem to have jobs, and were partying all the time. I just mucked in with everyone, found a space on the floor to kip down, and stayed there for a week and a half, as the whole town gradually came to fever pitch in anticipation of the long awaited Grand Prix. Not that anyone was particularly interested in the sport of motor racing, or professed to know much about Formula 1, but the consensus amongst Adelaideans was that this was just going to be one great big party.

In the week I was in Adelaide, I remember we all watched lots of MTV in the house, and for me one tune and iconic video will always be synonymous with where I was, and it is the timeless classic "Take On Me" by A-ha, which is not only a great tune, but it also has that brilliant pencil animation/live-action combination of a video which gave the band and the song huge exposure in October 1985, both in the States, and all around the world. So this was the background to the build up to the Grand Prix, and as all the posters described around town, "Adelaide Alive", this really was the place to be, to catch the action and join in with the craic, which is a good reason why it earns its place in this book.

Two years prior to the Adelaide Grand Prix, South Australia's Premier, John Bannon, had seen proposals for a race around the streets of Adelaide which had been put together by leading city tyre dealer, Bill O'Gorman, to coincide with Adelaide's 150th anniversary. Bannon liked the idea, but whilst Formula 1 boss Bernie Ecclestone's initial response was lukewarm, deeming Australia to be too far away, when two American venues backed out of the 1984 series, he changed his mind.

Bannon's event team was led by Mal Hemmerling, and he and his team quickly got into action and pulled together an exciting and entertaining event programme which would quickly become the benchmark for other Grand Prix venues around the world to follow. When Ecclestone and all the Formula 1 teams arrived in Adelaide in October 1985, two weeks after the South African Grand Prix, for the final round of the 1985 season, they were delighted with what they saw, and so were the drivers.

Double world champion Nelson Piquet led the plaudits, and speaking on behalf of his racing rivals, and having had initial concerns based on other recent experiences of street circuits, immediately offered a positive appraisal of the circuit when he said early in race week: "After Dallas and Las Vegas, we all expected another bad street circuit". Although the Adelaide circuit was temporary, it provided an attractive layout as it wound through the city streets, parkland, and also across Victoria Park racecourse, and unlike Monaco and Detroit with their endless short straights, narrow roads and tight corners, the Adelaide track was wide and very fast in places.

It also included a 900 metre long straight which was named after Australia's three time World Champion, Jack Brabham, where the faster cars could reach speeds of

200mph (322 km/h) and here, and unusually for a street circuit, there were opportunities for overtaking. So the reception for the circuit was excellent, as it was also for the very professional way in which the event had been organised. Remarkably this led to the promoters being awarded the Formula 1 Promotional Trophy in its inaugural year, and Ecclestone, in typically bullish tone, would go further and say that Adelaide had raised the standards of what was now expected of other venues, and other venues should take note or else.

The Race was scheduled to start at 2pm on Sunday 3rd November, and would comprise 82 laps of a 3.78 km circuit (2.362 miles) for a total race distance of 310 kilometres. First Qualifying would take place on Friday, and Final Qualifying on Saturday, and there was also an exciting schedule of Formula 3 and V8 Touring Cars to watch. On the Friday I ventured into town and tried to work out some decent vantage points for race day, and managed to gain general admission for free for the last half an hour, and saw Finland's Keke Rosberg take pole position by one hundredth of a second ahead of a young Brazilian driver called Ayrton Senna. There was now a tangible sense of excitement amongst the spectators around me, and undoubtedly this was very infectious, and I was definitely drawn in.

There were a number of previous World Champions in the field and these included the 1982 winner, Keke Rosberg, Nelson Piquet the 1981 and 1983 champion (he would go on to win a third title in 1987), and in the twilight of their careers, Niki Lauda, champion in 1975, 1977 and 1984, and also Australian Alan Jones who had won the drivers championship in 1980. And appropriately, Jones had been given the honour of driving the First Formula 1 car out onto the new track at the start of Q1 at 10am on the Friday morning.

French driver Alain Prost, after two very near misses in 1983 and 1984, enjoyed a dominant 1985 season, and had already been crowned 1985 champion before the cars lined up in Adelaide. By winning in 1985, Prost had become France's first ever Formula 1 World Champion, and he would go on to win four titles in all, the others being in 1986, 1989 and 1993, a period in which he and Ayrton Senna would develop a fierce rivalry. Other established names in the field included Jacques Laffite, Michele Alboreto and Riccardo Patrese, and exciting young drivers like Ayrton Senna, Gerhard Berger and Nigel Mansell, the latter who had won two weeks before in South Africa. Adding home interest to the proceedings, there were two other British drivers also in the starting line up, Martin Brundle and Derek Warwick.

My friend Sarah was working in the Hilton Hotel that week, so on the Saturday, we went into town together, so that I knew exactly where to pick her up from later in the evening, as we were then heading on to an "eve of race" party with friends whose house was situated on the corner of Flanders and Hutt Street, which was track side at turn 6. I wandered up to the circuit again that afternoon, and caught the back end of the V8 qualifying, which was again very exciting and noisy, as the cars were being thrown around the corners, back ends skidding all over the place.

The buzz was palpable after a thrilling Q2 session which had seen a battle royal between the Williams-Hondas of Keke Rosberg and Nigel Mansell, and the Lotus-Renault of Ayrton Senna. Mansell appeared to have taken pole position with an impressive time of 1:20.537, but late in the day, and out for his third and final run, Senna and his black and gold Lotus stunned everyone with a time of 1:19.843, seven-tenths faster than Mansell, and the only driver under 1 minute 20 seconds.

Although I missed Q2, I did manage to get track side for the last event of the day, the very entertaining Australian Touring Car championships finale. Touring cars had often been a support category for the Australian Grand Prix, but it was not until 1985 that it became an official supporting event. This was a thrilling spectacle as the V8 powered cars roared round the shortened track, and the race was won by Dick Johnson in a Ford Mustang GT. Unusually, Gerhard Berger, who was racing in the main event on Sunday for Arrows-BMW had successfully gained permission to race in this touring car event as well, though his BMW 635 Csi was unceremoniously spun off the track on lap three by local favourite John Harvey in his Holden Commodore. Lots of noise, screeching of tyres, plenty of incident, and for the many petrol heads, an absolute winner with the excitable crowd.

The eve of Grand Prix house party was a memorable occasion too! It was a black-tie party apparently, which was tricky on paper for me, because not surprisingly I didn't have anything smart in my backpack. However, I was loaned a black leather jacket, and thin black leather tie, and sported a blue shirt and a very short pair of white shorts,

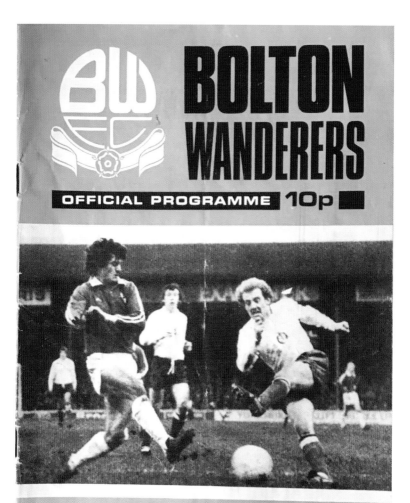

Match Day Programme for the FA Cup 5th round tie at Burnden Park,
Bolton Wanderers v Newcastle United, February 1976.
Note the programme price of 10p.

Geoff Boycott occupies the crease on his way to his 100th hundred at Headingley in 1977. I particularly like this image as Dad and I are in it, sitting on top of the long gone Winter Shed. *Courtesy of Getty Images - Patrick Eagar/Popperfoto*

The irrepressible Seve Ballesteros acknowledges the crowd at he captures his first Major at Royal Lytham in 1979.

Courtesy of Getty Images - Phil Sheldon/Popperfoto

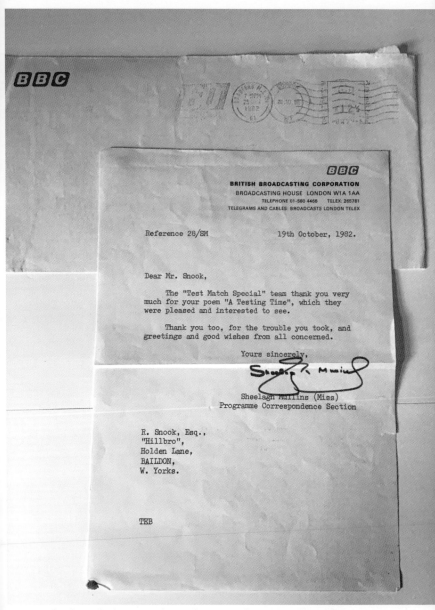

BBC

BRITISH BROADCASTING CORPORATION

BROADCASTING HOUSE LONDON W1A 1AA
TELEPHONE 01-580 4468   TELEX: 265781
TELEGRAMS AND CABLES: BROADCASTS LONDON TELEX

Reference 28/SM   19th October, 1982.

Dear Mr. Snook,

    The "Test Match Special" team thank you very much for your poem "A Testing Time", which they were pleased and interested to see.

    Thank you too, for the trouble you took, and greetings and good wishes from all concerned.

        Yours sincerely,

        Sheelagh Mullins (Miss)
        Programme Correspondence Section

R. Snook, Esq.,
"Hillbro",
Holden Lane,
BAILDON,
W. Yorks.

TEB

Letter of acknowledgement from the BBC who were pleased to receive my poem "Testing Time" which describes the unforgettable heroic deeds of Ian Botham and Bob Willis at Headingley 1981.

Tom Watson chipping at the 16th hole during the Seniors Open at Royal Birkdale In 2013, thirty years after his 5th and final Open Championship triumph at the same venue.   *Picture taken by James Snook*

112th OPEN
CHAMPIONSHIP
ROYAL BIRKDALE
1983

SUNDAY 17th JULY

STAFF

Admit to Course

TICKETS MUST BE DISPLAYED
AT ALL TIMES

No Dogs or Cameras

№   3453

The 1984-85 Bradford City team in celebratory mood - picture supplied by John Hendrie, which was taken an hour before the fire consumed the stand in the background.

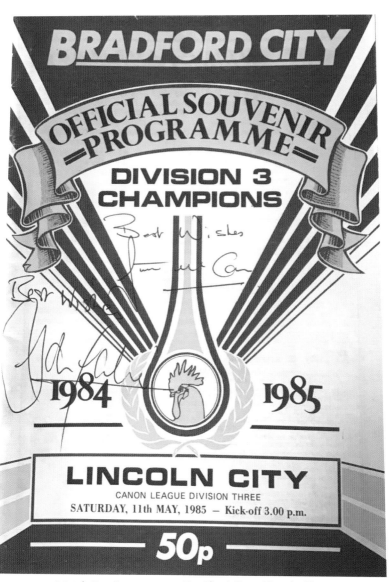

Match Day Programme - Bradford City v Lincoln City,
signed by Stuart McCall and John Hendrie.

'Broken Souls'
by Paul Town

In memory of the 56 loved ones we lost at Valley Parade, May 11th 1985
Always with us... Never forgotten
www.stadiumportraits.com

Limited edition print "Broken Souls" by Paul Town, in memory of the 56 fans who lost their lives at Valley Parade on May 11th 1985

Adelaide Alive Poster, courtesy of the Australian Grand Prix Corporation.
*(NB: this publication is not authorised or sponsored by the AGPC,
and does not represent the views of it)*

The capacity Yorkshire crowd thoroughly enjoying Royal Ascot in 2005. What a great spectacle, superbly captured by Tony Speight.

The pristine Parade Ring at York Racecourse, as owners, trainers, jockeys and horses prepare for the Gold Cup. *Image provided by Tony Speight.*

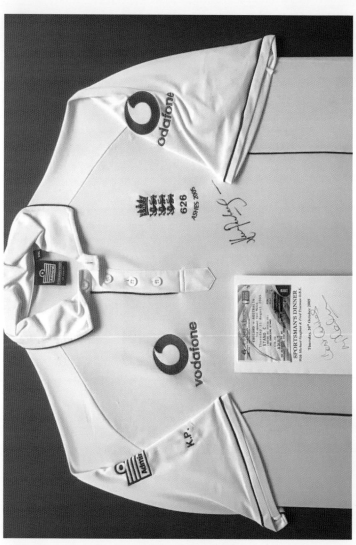

Ashes 2005: Each player was issued with 6 shirts for the series, and this is one of KP's, which Michael Vaughan auctioned at a Sportsman's Dinner – he also signed my menu card and ticket for the 1st day of the Old Trafford Test.

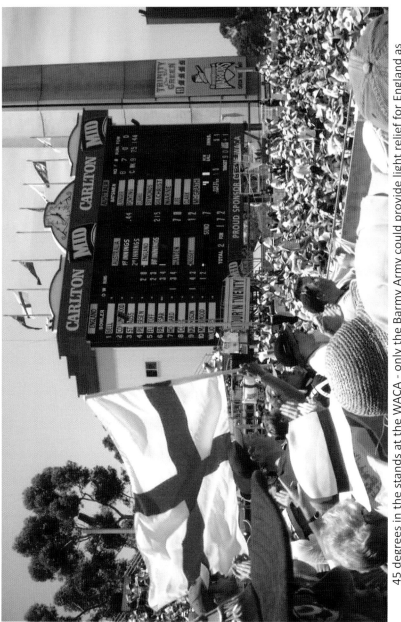

45 degrees in the stands at the WACA - only the Barmy Army could provide light relief for England as Adam Gilchrist blasted the second fastest Test century of all time.

London 2012 - just after the Men's hockey final, and with the Olympic Stadium in the background, the crowds gather at the BBC Tower hoping for a glimpse of Mo Farah.

Lords 2013 - England v Australia - the scorecard which highlights Joe Root's match winning 180, which I witnessed on a glorious sunny Saturday at the home of cricket.

This was my perfect birds eye view of the final Monday's play of the 2015 Open Championship at golf's spiritual home, St Andrews. *Image provided by Andrew Jennings.*

with white shoes. Another housemate called Lucy felt that my hair needed attention, and with the help of a bit of vaseline and hair curlers, she managed to produce a look all of its own. I did decline the offer of ear-rings and make up, but otherwise was ready to party! Sarah and I arrived at the party at 10pm, and it was already in full swing, and everyone was suffering from a serious case of race fever. I have never seen so much booze, and we had a brilliant evening, met some amazing people, and got home at 4.30am.

Race day dawned, and after 5 hours sleep we headed back down to the track, and the first glimpse of racing was in the historic cars category which was yet another popular novelty for the crowd, and it was great to see the cars of yesteryear roar down the long Dequetteville Terrace straight. I then worked my way around the circuit, past the start and finish area, past the Senna Chicane and then found a great spot very close to where the party had been held the night before at the Hutt Street corner. I figured this would be as good a place as any to install myself, as it was a pretty good viewing area, not too busy, it was free entry, and because it was a tight corner, the cars would slow down, so you could could see a lot more.

If you have never been to watch a Grand Prix live, there are a number of spectator experience suggestions I can suggest to you. Take a radio and listen to the race live as it happens, and use earphones to block out some of the noise. If I am being honest, after the first lap, it became increasingly difficult to know who was leading, and what the race order was; and so the other tip if going to watch, would be to sit opposite a giant screen, so you can also keep up to speed visually. All that being said, just being there was more than enough, and the whole experience was intoxicating.

The race started at 2pm, and Nigel Mansell took the lead at the start but on the first lap he and Senna collided, leading to Mansell's retirement. On an unforgiving track and in the 35 degrees heat, tyres became a constant problem, leading to many pit stops, and subsequent changes in race order. Keke Rosberg in his Williams-Honda and Ayrton Senna in his Lotus-Renault battled for the lead for much of the middle part of the race, but when Rosberg pitted for new tyres, he caught Senna by surprise, and the Brazilian went into the back of the Williams, resulting in Senna losing his front wing, and his having to pit two laps later.

Then it was Rosberg's turn to pit, but it was a slow stop, which allowed veteran Niki Lauda to lead the race for the first time, and what a story and fitting end to an extraordinary career it would have been if in his last race he was to carve out one final victory. However, two laps later Lauda's TAG Porsche had serious brake trouble and he had to retire on lap 58, safe at least in the knowledge that he had retired when leading his last Grand Prix. Senna was thus briefly back in the lead, but he too had to retire after an eventful race, when his engine started to smoke.

The race was now becoming attritional, and of the 25 starters on the grid, only eight cars finished, and only three of these managed to complete the full 82 lap distance. Rosberg now had time to pit again and his new tyres saw him safely through for what was his final Grand Prix victory, and the Ligier-Renault team of Jacques Laffite and Philippe Streiff from nowhere took second and third place, despite trying to bump each other out of the race on the final lap! To complete the points scorers, Ivan Capelli in the Tyrell was 4th, Stefan Johansson in a Ferrari 5th, and Gerhard Berger 6th in the Arrows.

The first Australian Grand Prix was over, Finn Keke Rosberg was crowned champion, and then the fans literally took it upon themselves to climb the barriers and walk on the track. I returned to Pauline's house where we had been the night before, and joined in the roof party which had suddenly sprung up at the end of the race, and fortified with plenty of left over grog, we were shouting down to everyone else who was still milling around walking the track, everyone in great spirits, enjoying the moment for every second it was worth.

In the early evening I made my way down to a large park with a lake inside the track where there were thousands of people enjoying the good weather, and the post-race entertainment which included a huge concert and a high-wire artist. Most people had had lots to drink and many were cooling off and diving into the lake. Meeting up with Sarah at the Hilton Hotel later on in the evening, and as I waited for her, one of the many celebrities in Adelaide that week, heavyweight boxer, Joe Bugner, stepped into a waiting Rolls Royce in front of me. I remember thinking that it would take Adelaide and its party loving folk a good few weeks to get back to normal after this. I was just happy to have been part of such an amazing week, the week when I saw Adelaide Alive!

"A Fever" (composed 1/11/1985)

Hailed by mail
To come without fail
Sarah social setter
Sent me that letter
So I strayed...
To Adelaide

Off we'd go
To the next show
On the fringe
Of a total binge
Meeting face after face
At Grand Prix pace

Once a gentle pace
Before the race
Now at a cost
Champion Prost
Takes on his friends
Over straights and bends

As a believer
With the fever
I was there
Without a care
In November 85
I saw Adelaide Alive

Adelaide continued to stage the Grand Prix up to and including 1995, and enjoyed its status as the traditional and exciting final round of the Formula 1 Driver's Championship. The drivers, their teams, and all the fans loved the location, the demanding circuit, and the craic that went with it, and after Rosberg's win in 1985, Alain Prost, Ayrton Senna and Gerhard Berger would each win twice, and Thierry Boutsen, Nelson Piquet, Nigel Mansell and Damon Hill once each. After some behind the scenes wheeler dealing between Bernie Ecclestone, and the Victorian Premier, and with some considerable bad-blood between the two rival States, the Australian Grand Prix moved to Albert Park, Melbourne, in 1996, where it is still staged to this day.

1985 was certainly Senna's breakthrough year, a season which saw him take no fewer than seven pole positions, which he converted into his first two of 41 career Grand Prix victories, winning both in Portugal and Belgium. Senna was on a very fast curve to greatness, a force of nature, undeniably fearless, competitive and very quick. There had been lots of talk about him in Adelaide as one to watch for the future, and I suppose there was no surprise that he would go on to dominate Formula 1, and become a multi-world champion. Three titles quickly followed for McLaren between 1988 and 1991, and he would win twice in Adelaide in 1991, and again in 1993.

Not that anyone knew then in 1993, but victory on Adelaide's by now famous street circuit would be Senna's final Formula 1 triumph, because the Brazilian who was still very much at the top of his sport, would suffer a fatal crash at the San Marino Grand Prix on May 1st 1994 aged just 34 years old. Fittingly, Senna had won his 65th pole position the day before and was leading the race when he crashed on the second racing lap. Telemetry data recovered after the crash showed that his car had entered the Tamburello corner at 309km/hour (192 mph), and after braking and exiting the corner, he hit the barrier wall at 211km/hour (131 mph). All of Brazil, and the world of motor racing would mourn the death of such a brilliant young talent.

In the eleven years that Adelaide held the Grand Prix there were many great moments to record. British fans will particularly recall the misfortune of Nigel Mansell in the 1986 race which cost him the Championship. Running third which was enough for him to win the title, he suffered a blown tyre on lap 63, allowing Prost to win his second title. The 1991 race was badly rain affected, and was the shortest Grand Prix in history, with only 14 laps being possible, resulting in half-points being awarded. And in 1994, the other year that the title was decided at the last race, Michael Schumacher and Damon Hill controversially collided on lap 35, and both had to retire, an outcome which favoured the German who would win his first driver's championship by a single point from the Englishman. Damon Hill would however win the final Adelaide Grand Prix in 1995 in front of a record crowd of 210,000 spectators, a fitting end for a hugely popular racing venue.

Chapter 9
Beware Bowlers Who Bat!

22nd – 26th November 1985
2nd Test: Sydney Cricket Ground:
Australia v New Zealand

The Grand Prix wasn't the only sporting attraction in Australia in 1985, and just two days later, the biggest annual horse race of the year in Australia, the Melbourne Cup, was taking place. I have no idea where Sarah and I got our stamina from but, after some late night packing, we arose bright and early on the Monday morning and were on the road at 6am hitching a lift to Melbourne.

After a slow start, we were very fortunate to find two amazing and completely contrasting lifts, that would take us all the way to Melbourne, where we would arrive nearly 14 hours later. The first hitch was in a big luxurious red Jaguar XJ 6, which took us in relative luxury about half way in just five hours, and dropped us off at the junction of the Great Ocean Road. After a good hour's wait, a camper van with five lads from Sydney stopped to pick us up. They were on tour for the Grand Prix and the Melbourne Cup and were great fun and only too happy to show us the sights of the Great Ocean Road, and the iconic 12 Apostles and London Bridge, the latter which has now fallen into the sea.

Having met up with more friends of Sarah's, we were driven north of the city to Templestowe, and as the following day was the Melbourne Cup, we had a public holiday to look forward to. Every metropolitan area of Melbourne, and indeed most of the State of Victoria takes a holiday on the first Tuesday in November to celebrate the annual running of Australia's most famous horse race, which has taken place every year since 1861 at the iconic Flemington Racecourse. The Melbourne Cup is the richest two-mile handicap race in the world and is known locally as the "race that stops the nation".

So we joined our hosts, Paul and Noel and their friends and so it seemed most of Templestowe at a local bar called Jim Finn's, where we enjoyed a very long lunch, and where we watched the famous race live on a giant screen with an increasingly noisy and expectant crowd. For the record the winner of what was the first million dollar Melbourne Cup was a New Zealand horse called "What a Nuisance", which in hindsight, and in the context of this chapter, could be said to have been portentous.

In 1985-1986, the New Zealand cricket team was touring Australia, and so there was some excellent cricket to watch as well. Whilst in Adelaide, I had managed to catch a day at the picturesque Adelaide Oval, where South Australia were playing the tourists in a warm up match which was memorable for the exceptionally talented Martin Crowe's

241 not out. The Adelaide Oval is much changed now, but is still a beautiful setting to watch cricket, surrounded as it is by green parks and church spires, on the banks of the River Torrens and with the iconic statue of Don Bradman to inspire you.

The two main characters at the heart of this chapter are however not batsmen, rather they are two New Zealand spin bowlers who surprised everyone by being able to bat a bit too. So we need to fast forward four weeks, and after the excitement of the Grand Prix and the Melbourne Cup, I had made my way to Sydney and high on my list of places to visit in Sydney, after the Harbour Bridge and the Opera House, was Sydney Cricket Ground, better known as the SCG.

Staying with a friend of a friend in a central suburb with a view of the Harbour Bridge, I soon worked out how to get to the SCG, where on Friday 22nd November, the second Test between Australia and Zealand was starting. When travelling alone and with an open ticket, you don't need to make any long term plans, so I felt this was a great opportunity to be an impartial observer at a Test match, and what better opportunity than this to watch all five days of a Test for the first, and probably the last time in my life. I am unashamedly a traditionalist when it comes to watching cricket, and whilst I enjoy watching all forms of the game, I still think that Test match cricket is still the ultimate form of the game.

The greatest rivalry between cricketing nations is undoubtedly the Ashes, but in the southern hemisphere, there is also a very intense Antipodean rivalry in all sports, especially rugby, but also cricket. This rivalry had been stoked by the disgraceful incident at the MCG in 1981 when on the instruction of his brother and skipper Greg, Trevor Chappell had bowled an underarm delivery to New Zealand batsman Brian McKechnie, thereby ensuring he could not hit a six off the final ball of the match. McKechnie calmly blocked the ball back and then angrily hurled his bat in the air in a display of utter disgust.

In an attempt to avert an international incident, the then Australian Prime Minister, Malcolm Fraser, called upon Greg Chappell to issue an apology, but his New Zealand counterpart, Robert Muldoon, was quick to stoke the fire by calling this an act of cowardice on the part of the Australian captain, and even quipped that he thought it was appropriate that the Australian team were wearing yellow.

Perhaps not surprisingly relations between players and supporters were still strained when the two sides met for a three match Test series just four years later. When you add into the mix the fact that New Zealand had never won a Test series in Australia, the stage was set for fireworks, and what a series this would turn out to be. Things got very interesting too when Richard Hadlee took 15 Australian wickets in the first Test at Brisbane, including career best figures of 9/52 in the first innings, and Martin Crowe hit 188 in the Kiwis' first innings, to secure an easy innings victory for the visitors.

So when the two teams met again ten days later in Sydney

for the second Test, there was a lot at stake, particularly for Australia. According to my diary entry I arrived at the SCG at 11.40am and perhaps surprisingly Australia, having won the toss, had asked New Zealand to bat first. At 79/0 at the lunch break, this looked to be a mistake as both openers, John Wright and Bruce Edgar, had batted sensibly and without too much alarm.

Then after lunch the spinners got to work, and in those days the SCG wickets had a reputation for helping slow bowlers, and veteran leg-spinner Bob Holland took full advantage and took six quick wickets. In addition, Martin Crowe, who had looked in imperious form was brilliantly run out by Greg Matthews and suddenly the Kiwis had collapsed to 169/9 with an hour of play still to go. This brought together New Zealand's last two batsmen, both in the team for their spin bowling, right arm off-spinner John Bracewell, and left arm slow orthodox, Stephen Boock.

Back in the 1980s the Sydney Cricket ground still had a large open grassed area for spectators to sit on, called "The Hill". It had a bit of a reputation for being rather lively, especially in the afternoon and evening sessions, and this was where I had decided to sit, and it was soon clear that the intense rivalry on the pitch was matched by Australian and New Zealand fans who were sat around me, and who traded mainly well meant and humorous banter, though in some instances fairly direct insults, for most of the day. I kept fairly quiet through the day, as I didn't want to give the Aussies any excuse to do some additional pommie bashing at my expense, and in any case they were happy Kiwi bashing instead.

In the midst of all the barracking, the New Zealand last pair somehow kept their nerve, and their wicket intact, and by the close of play the New Zealand score had advanced to 212/9 at stumps, an unbeaten stand of 43; John Bracewell, who was playing the senior role in the partnership, was 35 not out, and Stephen Boock was 11 not out. All in all it had been a very entertaining day's play characterized by tumbling New Zealand wickets, and despite a good start for the Kiwis, Australian captain Alan Border's decision to insert the opposition now appeared to have been a masterstroke.

Day two was set fair and I arrived in the ground about 15 minutes after the start of play, fully expecting to see Australia batting, particularly as the new ball was still only a few overs old, and whilst Bracewell was a decent batsman, the same could not be said of Boock who was a genuine number 11 batsman with a Test average of just over six. However, the New Zealand pair continued on their merry way, and having achieved the 50 partnership, runs began to come more freely, at which point the fielding side appeared suddenly desperate, which consequently made the home crowd restless.

A last wicket stand is always a frustration to the bowling side, who know that just one good delivery, or one poor shot will result in the end of the innings, but it is amazing how often the last pair of batsman can and do defy the odds. This leads to heightened interest on and off the field, and a tension that builds over by over. John Bracewell was particularly enjoying the stage, playing more and more expansively, and he reached his own 50, and the partnership rattled on to 100 runs.

How long could they carry on? Could the all time Test match record tenth wicket partnership held by fellow compatriots Brian Hastings and Richard Collinge made in 1973 against Pakistan of 151 runs be overtaken? The crowd sensed the approaching landmark, and the two batsmen, judging by their more uncertain stroke play, for the first time also became aware of it. Lunch was also approaching, and then finally with the score on 293, and having added 124 for the 10th wicket, Dave Gilbert trapped Stephen Boock leg before wicket for what would be his highest Test score in 41 innings of 37, leaving John Bracewell 83 not out. This unexpectedly protracted passage of play had come to a sudden end, which I suppose came as an anti-climax for impartial observers like me. Yet it had undoubtedly altered the course of the Test match allowing New Zealand unpredicted momentum, but how would the rest of the match play out?

Once again the afternoon's cricket was entertaining, both on and off the pitch! Saturday afternoon in the sunshine saw rival supporters lining up on either side of the Hill, as the drinking, joking, leering, jeering and barracking intensified and as the beer intake reached a peak, minor scuffles broke out, and police intervened in a sensible fashion to calm things down. All the while, Australia were fighting back having at one stage been in serious trouble losing their first five wickets for only 71 runs. New batsman Greg Ritchie was given a lifeline before scoring when New Zealand's wicket-keeper Ian Smith missed an easy stumping chance, and Australia closed the second day on 175/5, with Ritchie 60 not out and Greg Matthews 48 not out.

It was more of the same on day three, the middle Sunday of the contest. Richard Hadlee took five Australian wickets, and spinners Bracewell and Boock two a piece, as the home side were dismissed for 227, affording the visitors ascendancy and a first innings lead of 67. New Zealand extended their advantage with openers Wright and Edgar putting on exactly 100 for the first wicket. The light hearted barracking of the morning once again gave way to more determined and drunken chanting through the afternoon. "Hadlee's balls are better than yours" was followed by "Kiwis suck", then chanting of the words Kiwi, Aussie, ad nauseam. Then there followed a bout of can throwing and flag running. Often it was difficult to take your eyes off the crowd, easy to miss a wicket or a boundary. When play did end, the scoreboard showed that New Zealand were 119/3, and 186 runs ahead, and still definitely in the driving seat.

For the record, days four and five were rain affected, but the Aussie spinners, Holland, Bright and Matthews took nine wickets between them, scuttling New Zealand out for 193, setting Australia a challenging if smaller than expected target of 259 to win. Heavy rain stopped play mid-afternoon on the 4th day, with Australia 36/1. So the final days play was set up nicely, almost like a one day target, Australia requiring 229 to win with nine wickets remaining.

With rain intervening once again, a further hour was lost at the start of the final day, making the run chase tighter still for Australia. David Boon top scored for Australia with 81, but when he became Bracewell's third victim at 192/5, the match was once again very much in the balance, and what an opportunity for New Zealand to seize the momentum yet again in this fluctuating match. Unexpectedly, and with relative ease and in a very well judged 6th wicket partnership, David Hookes and Greg Matthews saw to it that the home side won by four wickets with just four overs left in the game.

Who says Test match cricket is boring. The outcome was in doubt right up to the very end. Bracewell and Boock's partnership was not quite enough to win the game, but it had given New Zealand fresh momentum, and it had been the fifth highest ever last wicket partnership in Test history. Despite ending up on the losing side, John Bracewell was awarded the man of the match for his 83 not out, and his five wickets in the match. All credit to Australia who despite batting last on a wearing spinning pitch, had squared the series when it mattered most.

The deciding Test in this three match series took place a week later at the WACA in Perth, Western Australia, and thanks to Richard Hadlee's dominance with the ball again, which saw him take 5/65 in Australia's first innings of 203 all out, and 6/90 in their second innings of 259 all out, New Zealand successfully chased down their target of 164 to win for the loss of just four wickets. Richard Hadlee's record return of 33 wickets in the three match series was pivotal, and New Zealand had beaten Australia in Australia for the first time ever by two Tests to one, an achievement which they have not been able to repeat since.

The Sydney Cricket Ground remains one of the most impressive sporting locations anywhere in the world. However, and in part because of a need to increase ground capacity, but also to sanitise spectator experience by removing the opportunity for boorish behaviour, the "Hill" area was replaced with concrete seating in the early 1990s, and the newly formed space was then formally named "Yabba's Hill" in honour of Stephen Harold Gascoigne, who was a well known pre-second world war heckler at the SCG.

Gascoigne was better known as "Yabba", and his colourful comments have made it into folklore, and these include of a fly-swatting England Bodyline captain Douglas Jardine... "leave our flies alone, Jardine. They're the only friends you've got here"... or to an opposition bowler... "your length's lousy, but you bowl a good width"... or to an English batsman adjusting his box between overs... "those are the only balls you've touched all day".

In 2007 the Doug Walter's stand and Yabba's Hill were demolished to make way for the new Victor Trumper stand, but to ensure that Australia's nostalgia of Yabba and the Hill lives on, and perhaps also to acknowledge the value of a good sledge, which we know the Australians love, a bronze statue depicting Yabba in characteristic pose delivering one of his famous interjections now adorns what once was the Hill area of the new stand.

Chapter 10
A Day at the Races

Royal Ascot comes to York
"Ladies" Day, June 14th, 2005

Ascot's racing heritage stretches back just over 300 years and the Royal meeting has become one of the most important fixtures in the sporting and social calendar. Ascot racecourse was founded in 1711 by Queen Anne, and the first race, Her Majesty's Plate with a purse of 100 guineas was first staged on August 11th of that year. Now a five-day event, the annual Flat Racing Festival is the present Queen's favourite meeting and has always been held at the traditional Berkshire venue, but because of a £185 million redevelopment it was moved 220 miles north to York Racecourse for the 2005 meeting.

The City of York has its own rich history, firstly as an important Roman settlement called Eboracum, then a Viking stronghold, and then the home of the Yorkists, and the famous White Rose. More infamously, and on the site of the present day racecourse, the Knavesmire once hosted public hangings, including that of England's most celebrated highwayman, Dick Turpin in 1739.

Richard Turpin, born in Essex in 1705, was a highwayman by trade, who assumed the alias John Palmer in 1737 to coincide with a move north to Yorkshire and presumably to create a new identity in a different part of the country. Ironically he was found guilty and executed for two counts of horse theft. Whilst his death by public hanging on the Knavesmire was by all accounts gruesome, Turpin's exploits would later be romanticised, most notably by the imaginary 200 mile ride from London to York on his trusty mare, Black Bess, which remains part of folklore to the present day.

Stretching even further back in time, Yorkshire lays claim to the oldest annual horse race in the English racing calendar. The Kiplingcotes Derby was first staged in 1519 and always takes place on the third Thursday in March, over an arduous four mile course of farm track and field close to the small hamlet of Kiplingcotes which is near the town of Market Weighton in the East Riding of Yorkshire.

The race is governed by a number of quirky ancient rules, one of which states that if the race is not run one year, then it must never be run again. Whilst the 2018 race was cancelled due to a waterlogged course, a single horse was led round the course to guarantee the future of the race. The 500th race took place as normal on 21st March 2019, and because of Covid-19, the 2020 race went ahead with only two riders and their horses (Ferkin and Harry), thereby preserving the race.

York's horseracing pedigree is impressive too. According to 19th century horse racing authority Robert Black, it is believed that Roman Emperor Septimus Severus introduced horse racing to York in the 3rd century. By the time racing had commenced on the present Knavesmire site in 1731, the sport of Kings was a big hit for racegoers of all social classes, and by the end of the decade, the August race week, known as the Ebor Festival, became the highlight of the city's calendar. York's horse racing architectural heritage is also second to none in as much as celebrated and pioneering northern architect John Carr, best known for Harewood House, also designed horse racing's first ever Grandstand at York Racecourse.

To this day, and following subsequent improvements over the last three centuries, York Racecourse remains one of the most beautiful and atmospheric venues to watch the "Sport of Kings". Spectators may choose to watch the racing from one of four impressive stands, The County Stand Enclosure, the Grandstand and Paddock and opposite, and on the other side of the track, the Clocktower Enclosure.

All these areas boast an abundance of bars and eateries to suit every taste, and the easily accessible racing area which includes an immaculately maintained Parade Ring and Winners Enclosure are all in easy reach of the finish line. Tote betting kiosks also abound, and in conjunction with the plethora of on-course bookies, punters have everything close to hand to ensure a memorable day at the races.

For those that enjoy a flutter on the horses, it's just a case then of backing the right horses, which is far more difficult than you might imagine. Inside knowledge is always highly sought after, and the average punter will either choose a horse for its name, or its number, or the reputation of the jockey, which works some of the time, but also increases the element of chance. Those that study form over a period of time are far more likely to be successful, but coming out with just a small profit is an achievement, and someone said to me once, even though you might be down on the day, always bet on the last race.

A day at York Races is a special day out, and for many years we ran a very successful corporate day for our clients on the Friday of the July John Smith's Cup meeting. We laid on a coach which arrived at the course at midday in time for a sumptuous and suitably wet lunch in a corporate marquee in the middle of the course, followed by a high tea at 4.30pm. In between, we enjoyed the racing, the craic, the Guinness and Champagne Bars, and hopefully won more than we lost on the nags. The coach would collect us at 6.30pm, and we were back in Leeds an hour later, and a very good time was had by all.

Of course attending Royal Ascot at York Races was on a totally different level. For starters, the Queen was there in person, and as is traditional, racegoers were asked to dress appropriately for the occasion, which means the Men are in top hat and tails, and the Ladies wear their best dresses, embellished with the latest millinery, large colourful hats, preferably those that don't blow away in the wind, or smaller but no less flamboyant fascinators.

There were eight in our party, and we and two other couples arranged for a friend with an eight seater vehicle to collect us in Ilkley and drive across to York, champagne en route, where we arrived about 12 noon, and met up with our other couple, who had driven there, and who had also transported a hand-made picnic of epic proportions thanks to the excellent provisions of Ben Rhydding's "The Red Pepper Deli" as it was then called. There was also half a case of chilled Laurent-Perrier champagne and lagers to wet our whistles.

We had about 90 minutes to enjoy our lunch before the Royal procession, and the first race at 2.30pm. So we took our time, kept the champagne flowing and studied the newspapers so that we might just be a little better informed about which horse to back. We were in good company, because rather like the Grand National meeting at Aintree, everyone else was doing the same thing, some standing, some having laid out tables, chairs, cutlery, flutes, but everyone doing it in style and dressed to the nines, and creating a jolly atmosphere. The forecast was not the best, and it was rather cold as well, so the alchohol and food were very welcome.

At about 1.30pm everyone packed away their lunches and started walking in convivial and expectant mood, all dressed in their glad rags, from the Bishopthorpe end of the course, rail side to the long finishing straight in the direction of the Grandstand enclosures.

This is when we first caught a glimpse of the Royal procession, a series of splendidly polished and turned out horse drawn carriages, making their way along the course in the same direction, the smiling Queen elegantly attired in a smart cream outfit with matching brown hat with feather and cream rim, the Duke at her side, the course lined with enthusiastic racegoers. The nearer we got to the

Grandstand area, the louder the buzz, and we settled in for the first race, bets placed, in anticipation of the off.

Yorkshire and Northern folk were there in their numbers to make the most of this one-time opportunity to rub shoulders with the Queen and create their very own Royal Ascot experience, and although overall numbers were down on the usual 300,000, York crammed in 220,000 spectators over the five days, and broke its own attendance record on Thursday's Ladies Day when 58,000 spectators were in attendance. Masta Plasta won the first race of the day, the Norfolk Stakes, and the biggest roar of the day was given to favourite Westerner who won the prestige race of the day, the Gold Cup, which is the oldest race of the Royal Ascot meeting, and is run over a marathon two and half miles, and is therefore a great test of stamina and attracts only the best stayers.

With the first race starting at 2.30pm, and the last race at 5.30pm, the action was pretty well non-stop, with barely enough time to check out the runners and riders in the parade ring, place your bets, relocate to your viewing place, and then hopefully to collect your winnings. It's always a very slick operation at York, and the noise of the crowd builds through the race, reserved and expectant at the start, but as soon as the horses hit the long finishing straight, the decibel levels rise gradually and reach fever pitch as the jockeys drive their horses to the winning line, and the commentator's voice on the loudspeaker is drowned out by the cacophony of noise. 58,000 people do make a lot of noise too, which certainly made this experience more exciting.

And then suddenly it's all quiet again, a hush descends on

the proceedings, as punters await clarification of the result, a particularly nervous moment in a close finish, or worse still if a photo finish is required. Of course there is nothing you can do to influence the result, but the wait merely adds a final element of theatre to the unfolding drama, and then the crackle of the loudspeaker is heard again, and the result is announced...."First Number 7, Second Number 1, Third Number 9 and Fourth Number 6"... at which point winning punters experience an adrenaline rush and head off to collect their winnings, whilst losing punters tear up their betting slips in their moment of anti-climax. And then half an hour later, it all starts again with the next race.

There must be a few people who go to the races and don't bet, but they are surely in the minority. The Irish are well known for the big stakes they put down, but equally lots of people will just put the minimum stake of £2 on each race, which means you are then invested in the outcome. Whether you bet on the nose or each way, it's great to get a winner or two, but win or lose, everyone is out to enjoy themselves, and there was a lot of people doing just that. Being Royal Ascot, and Ladies Day, everyone had also made a big effort to dress up, so whatever your background, rich or poor, male or female, all types were rubbing shoulders with each other and drinking in the infectious atmosphere. There were some very interesting sights as well as the day drew on!

When the racing was over, and the on course bookies were busy packing up and counting their profits, the reluctant to leave punters are invited to partake in another of Royal Ascot's traditions of "singing around the bandstand". The community singing idea was first brought in during the

1970s, and was an immediate hit with racegoers, and has remained an integral part and finale to each and every day of the meeting since then.

It was certainly a big hit with the thousands at York who, song sheets in hand and all inhibitions long abandoned, were only too pleased to take part in the singing of a series of well known British favourites. There were at least 20 band members all immaculately dressed in bright red uniform, playing their wind and brass instruments for all they were worth, led by an inevitably eccentric band leader, who was resplendent in his white jacket, boater in one hand, whilst conducting the crowd by waving a large flag of St George in the other. Plenty of Pomp and Circumstance, with a bit of My Bonnie Lies Over the Ocean culminating in a patriotic outpouring of the National Anthem.

What a great day we had doing our very own take on Royal Ascot, and we left the Knavesmire in great spirits, found our chauffeur Andy very easily, and we were soon out of the traffic, having found a quieter route adjacent to the busier A64, where we happened across a surprising and bizarre sight, which was totally incongruous with "Ladies" Day at Royal Ascot.

For there on the road side, was a stationary minibus, and a woman squatting beside it, dress held up, hat still on, holding her handbag, relieving herself in full view of her friends, and for that matter all and sundry. The lady just didn't bat an eyelid at her very public display, and was loudly cackling with her mates. You couldn't make it up could you, and it would probably only happen up North, but we have a saying here: "when you gotta go, you gotta go"!

Chapter 11
The Greatest Match Ever Drawn?

Old Trafford, 11th August 2005, 3rd Ashes Test

The greatest and most enduring rivalry in cricket is the Ashes which is a biennial Test cricket series played on an alternating home and away basis between England and Australia. First played in 1877, the term 'Ashes' came into being in 1882 when England lost a one Test series at home for the first time in a very low scoring match at the Oval. A mock obituary was then posted in the Sporting Times declaring the death of English cricket, which stated that "the body will be cremated and the ashes taken to Australia". The Honourable Ivo Bligh adopted the term and, as captain of the English team that travelled to Australia the following winter, he promised to bring the "Ashes" home. The so called "Ashes" are housed in a tiny wooden urn, and ironically the smallest trophy in World Sport is arguably cricket's biggest prize.

Up to and including the most recent series played in England in 2019 which was one of only six drawn series, and since the inaugural Test in 1882/3, Australia has won 32 to England's 31 series. The contest has known great controversy, as well as great deeds, from the depths of the Bodyline series in 1932-1933 which caused a seismic international diplomatic furore because of England's ungentlemanly tactics (bowling at the batsman's body), to the daring deeds of Ben Stokes' heroic match winning innings at Headingley in 2019.

Cricket commentators, observers, fans and players from all over the world agree that there is one cricket series that stands out above all others, and that was the 2005 Ashes series played in England. Leading into the series, England had suffered eight straight series defeats from 1989 to 2002/3, and such had been Australia's dominance in this period, England had managed only seven Test wins to Australia's twenty-eight.

This would be Ricky Ponting's first Ashes series as captain, but his experienced team was well clear at the top of the World Test rankings, and were odds on favourites to continue their winning streak. Yorkshire and England's Michael Vaughan was also captaining his first Ashes series, and although the England team had suffered a heavy 4-1 series defeat down under in 2002/3, Vaughan had emerged as England's best batsman from that tour, scoring three big centuries, which also earned him Player of the Series. Could Vaughan and his team win the Ashes back after such a lean run?

Before the Test Series got underway, the two teams contested a one off T20 match, and then a 50 over NatWest series with Bangladesh, and there was clear evidence that England would seek to play in a more aggressive manner and they claimed an early psychological advantage when they dismissed Australia for just 79 to win the T20 with ease.

South African born Kevin Pietersen, an exciting but largely unknown talent had qualified to play for England in 2004, and was quickly brought into the England International set up, and immediately caught the eye by scoring a match winning 91 not out to win their first 50 over contest, and when England and Australia met in the final, a low scoring game ended in a tie, and the trophy was shared. The early sparring was over, and the hopes of England fans had been raised but, as ever, one Australian player, Glenn McGrath, unsurprisingly predicted a 5-0 Test series win for his team.

The first Test was played at Lord's and got off to an explosive start. Ricky Ponting won the toss and elected to bat, and was soon in the wars when he was hit and had his cheek cut by a rapidly rising delivery from England's fastest bowler Steve Harmison, who was under clear instructions from Vaughan to make his mark. Harmison rattled the Aussies and took 5/43 as the visitors were bowled out for 190 in just 40 overs. Not to be out done Glenn McGrath responded brilliantly taking the first five England wickets himself as the home side were reduced to 21/5 and closed a breathless days play which had seen no fewer than 17 wickets fall on a dispiriting 92/7.

Kevin Pietersen was making his Test debut and despite the perilous state of the scoreboard, he took the attack to the Australian bowlers on the second morning, and reached a maiden 50, raising England's total to a still disappointing but at least more respectable 155 all out. Australia quickly resumed normal service in their second innings, Michael Clarke top scoring with 91, as they reached 384 all out setting England an unlikely 420 to win, and although Pietersen ended up on 64 not out he ran out of partners, and Australia had triumphed by the huge margin of 239 runs. Australia had survived England's early shock tactics to take a 1-0 series lead, and the press were quick to turn against England.

Two weeks later the teams met again in the second Test at one of England's most successful Test venues, Edgbaston. Australia had been happy to talk things up before the game, and tried to pile psychological pressure on England's top order batsmen, and when Ricky Ponting won a second consecutive toss, he had no hesitation in asking England to bat, this despite losing his star opening bowler Glenn McGrath thirty minutes before the start of play when he accidentally stood on a cricket ball during final warm up and tore his ankle ligaments.

England, buoyed by McGrath's absence, took full advantage of being inserted, and became the first team to score 400 runs on the first day of a Test since 1938, with free flowing opener Marcus Trescothick starring with a scintillating 90 off just 102 balls which included 15 fours to set the pace of the day. Kevin Pietersen again with 71 and Andrew Flintoff with 68 continued the assault, and England were dismissed for 407 at the end of a pulsating day's play. On the second day, Australia reached 262/5 at one stage in their reply, but were dismissed for 308, and England closed on 25/1.

Australia bounced back and reduced England to 75/6 in their second innings before fireworks from England's flamboyant all rounder Andrew Flintoff shifted the momentum back to England. His aggressive innings of 73 included four big 6's, but even still England were dismissed for 182, setting Australia 282 to win. The remainder of another breathless days cricket was all England's as Flintoff toiled away and it climaxed with the dismissal of the dangerous Michael Clarke who was fooled by a cleverly disguised slower ball by Steve Harmison, and Australia ended the day 175/8, still needing 107 runs to win, but with only two wickets in hand.

England were on the brink of victory, but as is often the case with Ashes matches, there was still a twist in the tale. Shane Warne and Brett Lee continued to prosper well into the morning of the 4th day, and added 45 for the 9th wicket, before Warne hit his own wicket off Flintoff, when the score was 220. With 61 still required to win, Brett Lee was joined by McGrath's replacement and No. 11 batsman, Michael Kasprowicz, and the two of them defied the odds and took the score closer and closer to the target which only an hour ago had appeared such a long way off.

In one of the most nerve wrenching finishes to a Test match, which saw one of Flintoff's deliveries going for five no balls to reduce the deficit to nine to win, Michael Vaughan kept faith with his quickest bowler one final time, and with only three runs needed to win, Steve Harmison produced another short ball, which if truth be told was not that well directed, but it induced Kasprowicz to take evasive action and with one hand on and one hand off the bat he gloved it down the leg side, wicket-keeper Geraint Jones took the catch, umpire Billy Bowden raised his crooked finger, and Edgbaston and the whole country breathed an enormous sigh of relief, and England were back on level terms in the series.

England had won by two runs, which was and still is the second narrowest margin of victory in Test history. This was definitely the moment that re-launched England's hopes; defeat and a 2-0 deficit would have been curtains for England. Australia's gamble had back fired, and the psychological battle and the momentum in the series had suddenly shifted, the press were now on England's side (Flintoff was dressed in a cape in the role as superhero in one newspaper) and the interest levels amongst the public went ballistic.

Back to back Test matches meant that there were only four days for the fans to wait before the next chapter was written, and the best news of all was that we had tickets for the first days play at Old Trafford on Thursday 11th August. I say we, because I was taking my 12 year old son James, and my 13 year old godson Oliver, and his Australian father "Gilly". I am sure that sharing great live sporting moments with family and friends is another important part of the enjoyment factor, and certainly makes it all the more memorable.

Gilly and Oliver drove up from Nottingham the night before, and we all headed off nice and early to drive over the Pennines to Manchester for the big day. We parked at one of the outlying stations and took the train the short distance to Old Trafford station which is next to the ground, and immediately joined a throng of expectant spectators, all carrying bags full to the brim with their packed lunches, mostly home supporters, but Gilly who was wearing his West Coast Eagles shirt was quickly into conversation with other like minded Aussies too. The banter had already started!

Thankfully the weather was set fair too, and we made it into the ground in good time, to see the teams finish their warm ups, and although the ground was not full, there was a huge roar when Michael Vaughan won his first toss of the series, and without hesitation elected to bat. England fans at least were more than happy with this outcome, and the atmosphere built nicely to the sounds of Jerusalem. England were unchanged, and despite pre-match concerns over the fitness of both Aussie quicks Glenn McGrath and Brett Lee, both were passed fit to play, and would be opening the bowling.

The nation was awash with Ashes fever after the thriller at Edgbaston, and by batting first on a glorious sunny day, England now had the ideal opportunity to create some momentum. However, England got off to a shaky start, as Trescothick was dropped by Gilchrist, and Strauss was then hit in the helmet by Lee, before being bowled by the same bowler with a clever slower Yorker. This brought England's skipper Michael Vaughan to the crease, and short of runs as he was, he needed to play a big innings here, but he initially looked nervous, and his footwork was tentative, his first scoring shot being a streaky boundary through gully off Gillespie.

After the first hour's play, Vaughan and particularly Trescothick began to play more freely. Trescothick was never blessed with the best footwork himself, but had a wonderful eye, and it was in today, and there were a number of sweetly struck boundaries, but just as Vaughan was beginning to look set and had reached 41, he had two lives in two balls, off the luckless McGrath. Firstly he chased a wide ball and edged it, only for wicket-keeper Gilchrist to tip it over the bar so to speak, and then the next ball he was bowled all ends up, only for umpire Steve Bucknor to signal NO BALL. McGrath's rueful smile said it all.

Trescothick reached his 50 in the next over, and England prospered either side of lunch, Vaughan having been reprieved, now playing with greater freedom like the natural stroke maker he was. The score had reached 163/1 when Trescothick swept at leg spinner Shane Warne and the ball seemed to go down into the ground, and then ricochet backwards and upwards to be caught by keeper Gilchrist, and after an eerie silence, Trescothick was given out. An unusual dismissal, but a memorable one for Warne, and it was a special moment for everyone in the crowd to witness this landmark achievement, the first bowler to capture 600 wickets in Test history. Warne raised the ball to all parts of the ground, and received genuine and unanimous applause from both Australian and English fans.

Michael Vaughan now moved into overdrive, and gave the crowd a masterclass in timing and all round stroke play. A positive leg-side clip off McGrath brought up his 15th Test century, and his fourth against Australia, and his first in England. He did give one more chance off Warne but was dropped by Hayden at slip, before accelerating to his 150 with some imperious drives, square cuts, and one swivel pull off Jason Gillespie for six which particularly sticks in the mind.

The Australians turned to part time spinner Simon Katich and despite bowling a juicy full toss, Vaughan, to everyone's surprise, not least his own, and with the opportunity of a double century at his mercy, tamely holed out at long on for a majestic 166. He walked off the ground to an amazing ovation, having stamped his mark on the series, in the knowledge that at 290/3 England were in a very strong position. The day ended with a flurry of runs from Ian Bell who scored his first Test 50 against Australia, and Kevin Pietersen, who scored a quick cameo 21 before holing out on the boundary to the new ball bowling of speedster Brett Lee. England closed the day on 341/5, and it had been another brilliantly entertaining day of cricket, and thankfully we had been there to see the England captain in full flow.

It had been England's day; Gilly and Oliver were slightly less enthusiastic than James and I were at the close of play, but we had all enjoyed each others company, the atmosphere, the weather, the action, lunch and tea. The crowd banter had been good all day, and in particular Jason Gillespie, who had badly misfielded in front of us, copped for a lot of stick throughout the day. Being a young and budding leg-spinner himself, my son James particularly enjoyed seeing Shane Warne bowl, and also the moment when he took his 600th Test wicket.

Shane Warne was that rarity in international cricket, a slightly portly, spiky blonde haired and supremely confident individual who could change a match in a moment of brilliance, who was unorthodox with both bat and ball, and someone who was happy to ruffle feathers, and never shied away from a contest. He would play a huge part in this series taking 40 wickets at an average of just under 20, and in this Test match scoring a belligerent 90 in Australia's first innings reply, which despite Simon Jones's excellent return of 6/53 meant Australia avoided having to follow on. Remarkably for a lower order batsman, and because of a long rain delay on the middle Saturday of the Test, Warne would also bat on all four of the final 4 days of the match.

In reply to England's 444 all out, Australia made 302, and in their second innings, England batted aggressively again, and despite being hit for a second time in the match by Brett Lee, which drew blood from his ear, Andrew Strauss led the way with an exciting 106, allowing England to declare late on the fourth day on 280/6, which left Australia about 100 overs to score an unlikely 423 to win, which was reduced by the Australian openers to 399 as they survived a 10 over spell. Much more likely was an England win, and the nation sensed another victory was on the cards.

Most Test matches either do not go to a fifth and final day, or if they do, prospects for a full days play and an England victory are typically low. However, and given the excitement that was growing in this series, and with the promise of heavily discounted admission prices of £10 for adults and £5 for children as well, all was set for a big final day. No one seemed to anticipate the heightened interest levels, but such was the mood of the nation, that many queued up overnight for the chance to purchase tickets, and Lancashire's chief executive simply said "I've never seen anything like it".

The following morning saw long queues forming outside Old Trafford as fans gathered in the hope of getting a ticket from as early as 3.30am. By 7am queues had stretched all around the ground, and when the players arrived, both teams needed police escorts to get to the ground. By 9am all 19,000 available tickets had been sold, and it was estimated that there were over 10,000 people locked out and unable to gain entry.

Lancashire's marketing manager Geoff Durbin said: "It's unbelievable the heights cricket can reach – at the moment it's even putting soccer in the shade. The only disappointment is that we have had to lock the gates and turn away so many people." The players were only too aware of these announcements, and Andrew Strauss summed up the mood of the players, saying on the one hand how much they were all lifted by the public's interest in the series, but also how much added pressure this put on the players as they took to the field.

The final day's play did not disappoint either, and the result would be in the balance all day, and as it turned out those spectators lucky enough to get in would not know the result until the last ball of the final 98th over of the day had been bowled. This would prove to be yet another epic climax, as England tried to take 10 wickets, and as Australia tried to avoid defeat.

With a packed partisan crowd eager for the action, England could not have got off to a better start when opener Justin Langer nicked off to Matthew Hoggard's first ball of the day, and in front of his home crowd, Freddie Flintoff produced a fearsome spell of fast bowling which finally accounted for Hayden for 36. But with skipper Ricky Ponting looking very assured, and the pitch still playing well, Australia reached lunch in a promising position of 121/2.

Damien Martyn was unfortunate to be adjudged leg before wicket to Steve Harmison, but when Flintoff prized out left handers Simon Katich and then Adam Gilchrist, Australia were 182/5, and England were back in the ascendancy. Ricky Ponting was clearly enjoying the theatre and cruised to his 23rd Test match century, but when Clarke fell to Jones offering no shot, and Gillespie to Hoggard for no score, England just needed three more wickets to win. Once again Shane Warne frustrated the England bowlers scoring a typically unorthodox 34, but he too fell to Flintoff, in bizarre fashion. He edged to Strauss at second slip, but Strauss never even got hands on it, but as luck would have it the ball bounced off his thighs and wicket keeper Jones leapt sideways to scoop a sensational rebound catch.

The crowd let off collective steam and as Mark Nicholas described it: "The lid is coming off the ground here in Manchester". England now needed two wickets, but only had eight more overs to do it. With just four overs remaining, skipper Ponting tried to pull Steve Harmison again but this time got a glove on the ball, and was caught by Geraint Jones, and now the crowd really went crazy because victory was finally in sight. The Australian skipper was crestfallen, and believing the match was now probably lost, could not raise his bat despite the richly deserved standing ovation he received for his superb innings of 156.

Out to the middle came last man standing Glenn McGrath to face the music of England's fired up quick bowlers, Flintoff and Harmison, with the nearly hero of Edgbaston Brett Lee once again at the other end. There were a number of close calls, and then it came down to the last over of the day, and Harmison again. Somehow McGrath survived the first two balls of the over, and pushed a single off the third ball, leaving Brett Lee to survive the last three balls. And then there was just one ball left, and trying for a Yorker, Harmison bowled a full toss which Lee played back calmly enough. Arms held aloft, this was redemption for the courageous Brett Lee who just a few days earlier had needed the big arm of sympathy from Flintoff at Edgbaston.

The Australian balcony erupted in delight and celebrated the moment like it was a victory; When interviewed afterwards a happy Brett Lee joked that " I don't think I can handle this anymore", and when Mike Atherton interviewed Michael Vaughan after the game he opened by saying " you have just given the nation collective heart failure". Vaughan remained positive and said what a great game of cricket it had been, and praised his team for another excellent performance, but England must have been mightily disappointed not to win the match.

Michael Vaughan had however at this crucial moment of the series spotted the opposition's weakness, and calling his team into a huddle before they left the pitch, he drew their attention to the manner of the Australian balcony celebrations, which were commensurate with a victory, not a draw. Vaughan's astute captaincy now came to the fore, and in the knowledge of what he had just witnessed, he confidently explained that England now had the match of the Australians and predicted ultimate victory. Apparently his words of wisdom went something like this... "we've got them by the ding dang doos, and we are going to win the series."

No doubt about it, the long rain delay on the third day had saved Australia on this occasion. However, because of it we were treated to a thrilling final day of the Test match, which, frustrating as the result was for England supporters, will live long in the memories of those who were there. As will that exhilarating first day performance by England, and Vaughan's splendid 166, which was a pleasure to witness, and which allowed my son and I and our Australian friends a ring side seat at the greatest series ever played. Surely this Old Trafford Test was the greatest Drawn Test of all time?

The postscript to Old Trafford was perhaps not surprisingly two more thrilling encounters against the old enemy. Trent Bridge was the venue for the 4th Test, and England were delighted to hear that both Glenn McGrath and Jason Gillespie were left out of the Australian side, and winning a second toss in a row, the England captain chose to bat first again, and on a rain affected first day, England reached 229/4 at the close, Michael Vaughan once again being dismissed by a part time bowler for 58, this time by opposing skipper Ricky Ponting.

Kevin Pietersen was dismissed early on day two, but then Andrew Flintoff and keeper Geraint Jones took the fight to the Australians and added 177 runs for the seventh wicket, Flintoff with 14 boundaries leading the way and reaching a first century against Australia, and when he was out for 102, Jones took over the role of aggressor and scored 85. England had rallied strongly and were all out for tea for 477. By stumps, and with Hoggard finding plenty of swing, Australia had slumped to 99/5, and were all out the next day for 218, with Simon Jones the pick of the bowlers, with another five wicket haul, picking up 5/44.

Seeing that Australia were still 259 runs behind, Michael Vaughan gambled on enforcing the follow on, as much to impress a psychological impact on his opposition, after all they had not followed on in their previous 190 Tests over a 17 year period.

Australia ended the day on 222/4, Ricky Ponting having been run out by substitute fielder Gary Pratt, who was on for the injured Simon Jones, the latter who would play no further part in the series. The Australian captain was particularly annoyed with the manner of his dismissal, having already been unhappy with England's tactic of using specialist fielders as substitutes, and his angry reaction appeared to gift England another psychological boost. Australia's middle and lower order made life very difficult for England's tiring and depleted bowling attack, and were finally all out for 387 on the fourth day, setting England a modest 129 to win.

As has previously been written, small targets are not always easy to reach, and despite a positive start by England's openers, as soon as Shane Warne came on to bowl, things changed quickly, and at 57/4 and then 116/7, the result was in the balance. England now had to rely on the bowlers to get over the line, one of whom, Simon Jones was injured. England just needed 13 more runs, but the scoreboard was stuck as Ashley Giles and Matthew Hoggard nervously played at Warne and Lee, but when Hoggard produced an unexpected cover drive for four off Brett Lee, the pressure was lifted, and Giles clipped Warne through mid-wicket for the winning runs, and just as Michael Vaughan had predicted, England were now 2-1 up in the series.

After three back to back nerve jangling Test matches, the sides went to the Oval for the fifth and final deciding Test. If England avoided defeat, the Ashes would be theirs for the first time since 1986, but if Australia won, they would level the series and by doing so retain the Ashes. Despite it being a working day, 7.4 million people watched the first day's play on Channel 4 – more evidence that the nation was gripped!

Vaughan won another crucial toss much to the delight of the partisan crowd, and England posted 377 all out thanks to 129 from Andrew Strauss and 72 from Freddie Flintoff, Shane Warne picking up 6/122. In reply Australia almost matched England, and were all out for 367, having at one stage been 185/0, with openers Langer and Hayden both scoring centuries, but oddly coming off for bad light after tea on day two, and thereby losing crucial time in the match. Flintoff again led England's bowling attack taking 5/76, and Hoggard picked up 4/97.

The game was finely balanced at the start of the fifth day with England only 40 runs ahead, and nine wickets in hand.

McGrath and Warne made inroads in the morning, and at lunch England were still precariously placed at 133/5. Kevin Pietersen had been visibly shaken up by a couple of fearsome short balls, and only just avoided losing his wicket and needed Vaughan's reassurance during the luncheon break.

After lunch, England and Pietersen came out all guns blazing, and helped by some uncharacteristic dropped catches, most notably by Warne at second slip, Pietersen then smashed his way to his first Test century in a manner that had the crowd on their feet most of the afternoon, and when he was finally out for 158, having hit 14 fours and seven sixes, he had added 122 with Ashley Giles, who would bat on and make a 50 of his own. There was not enough time for Australia to overtake England, and despite a theatrical delay due to bad light, when finally umpire Rudi Koertzen dislodged the bails, England's victory was confirmed. The Ashes had been regained at long last, in a style befitting of such an extraordinary five Test series.

The Nation had been gripped throughout, and Vaughan and his team were suddenly feted as national heroes, and after what can only have been a long night of celebrations, the following day they had the opportunity to thank the public for their support as they enjoyed an open top bus parade around London. By his own admission England's captain said "there was a lot of insecurity in the team", and that at times he had "blagged it", but to this day he still gets people coming up to him saying "they were inspired to take up cricket because of 2005." That surely is the acid test of just how big a series this really was, and one wonders whether there will ever be a series to compare.

Chapter 12
Doctor Needed!

WACA: 3rd Ashes Test, 16th December 2006: Gilchrist on Fire!

The incredible 2005 Ashes series had gripped a nation and restored national pride, and whilst Ricky Ponting's captaincy had been heavily criticised back in Australia, the England team had enjoyed all the trappings that go with a long awaited victory, including the open top bus parade, a reception at Downing Street, and then OBEs for skipper Michael Vaughan and coach Duncan Fletcher, and MBEs for all the players in the 2006 New Year's Honours List.

Another welcome consequence of England's success was a surge in popularity for cricket, and with only 14 months to wait before England toured Australia, anticipation here and in Australia was high. However, as the teams prepared for the return 2006/7 series, England were badly affected by injuries, with skipper Michael Vaughan and reverse swing expert Simon Jones both missing. Vaughan's character and leadership had been crucial to the win in 2005, and in his absence first Andrew Strauss and then

Andrew Flintoff had each been given a trial three match home series as captain.

Apparently Flintoff had been promised the captaincy for the tour of Australia which was certainly a high risk strategy on the part of the England Management Team. Could the hero of 2005 cope with the demands of being England's go to player with bat and ball, as well as the additional burden of the captaincy? In hindsight, this decision would turn out to be just one of a number of mistakes leading into the Tour, and the stronger candidate for the captaincy, Andrew Strauss would have to wait four long years to get his chance to captain an Ashes tour in Australia.

There were other cracks appearing in the England ranks, which would derail their best laid plans after they had arrived in Australia. Marcus Trescothick had to return home before the first Test started due to a recurrence of a stress-related illness, and Ashley Giles would also have to return home mid-tour as his wife had been diagnosed with a brain tumour. In contrast Australia, under a more determined than ever Ricky Ponting, was leaving no stone unturned in their pursuit of regaining the Ashes, a series which would also coincide with the retirement of Shane Warne, Glenn McGrath, Damien Martyn and Justin Langer, all of whom were desperate to go out on a high.

If the preparations for both sides were vastly different, the press and public were not holding back on placing great expectations on both teams. On the eve of the series, Ricky Ponting again faced criticism from his own press for his failings in 2005, whilst Andrew Flintoff was eager to play up the contest when he commented "...we are going over there to play in what could be the biggest series ever so there is an excited group of lads...", but he also went on to strike a note of reality.... "it is going to be tough, and we know that 2005 was something special and whether that can be recreated I am not quite sure... in England each Test match got bigger and bigger and we got a real feeling of what the Ashes was about".

The Sydney Morning Herald newspaper described the series as "the most anticipated Ashes ever", and tickets went on sale to the general public nearly six months in advance of the 1st Test, and were sold out within two hours for all five Tests. This certainly made life difficult for me, as I was hoping to purchase tickets for the 3rd Test in Perth, which would be the first destination of many for a long awaited three week family holiday down under for my wife Emma, now 14 year old son James, and our 11 year old daughter Joanna.

We were all set to fly out of Heathrow late on the 13th December, and would arrive just as the second day of the 3rd Test was starting. Travel plans were all in place when a good friend and work colleague of mine encouraged me to phone in to BBC 5 Live Radio and to apply to be a reporter for the Perth Test. In response to the anticipation of yet another thrilling Ashes series, in late November the BBC ran a competition to find a "roving reporter" for each of the five Tests, and as we would be in Perth at the right time, I plucked up courage, rang the BBC, was rung back the following day on the Victoria Derbyshire show, and was given a minute to explain why I should be considered for the role.

I was mightily surprised to be called back two days later to say that I had got the gig! This prompted me to renew my search for match tickets, and the only possible means of obtaining tickets so late in the day was to go through the Barmy Army, and because there were four of us, I needed four tickets. There was still availability, but there was one additional snag to overcome, in that I had to buy tickets for each of the first four days of the Test, which meant I had to buy 16 tickets in total, and find £1,600 overnight. The tickets were duly purchased, and fortunately my former dentist, David, now living in Perth, was only too pleased to take the first, second and fourth day tickets, and would also collect them, and pay me in cash for them when we met up with his family on the Friday night.

By this time, England had already lost the first Test at the Gabba in Brisbane, where Steve Harmison had bowled a wide to captain Flintoff at second slip with the first ball of the series, and Ricky Ponting had stamped his authority on proceedings by scoring a brilliant 196, thereby setting the tone for the series. England could only manage to take 10 Australian wickets in the entire match, and were heavily beaten by the margin of 277 runs.

There was therefore a lot resting on the second Test at Adelaide, and England's luck appeared to have changed, as they won the toss and posted a formidable 551/6 declared, with Paul Collingwood scoring 206 and Kevin Pietersen 158, the pair putting on 310 for the fourth wicket. Ashley Giles crucially dropped a catch to allow Ponting a life, and he and Clarke went on to score big 100s to post 513 all out, this despite a courageous bowling performance by Yorkshire's Matthew Hoggard, who took 7/109.

England were comfortably placed at 59/1 at the close of day four, and a draw seemed inevitable. However, Shane Warne, who had the surprisingly poor bowling figures of 1/167 in the first innings, had the last laugh as he turned the match on its head by taking four quick second innings wickets on the final morning, which saw England collapse in just 20 overs to 129 all out. Australia could not believe their luck and had ample time to reach their target of 168 to secure an unexpected six wicket win, and deal a terrible psychological blow to the England team and to their aspirations.

A few days before our departure, the BBC sent me a package which contained a palm device, (a hand held computer, which I suppose was the precursor to the smartphone), and instructions how to use it, which would allow me to send back daily reports on the cricket to London. Already 2-0 down in the series, and having suffered a very damaging defeat in Adelaide, England now faced an uphill struggle to stay in the series, and next up was the third Test at the WACA, Perth, where England had only ever won one Test before, a ground that Australians considered to be a fortress. This then was the stark cricketing reality that we were met with on our arrival into Australia.

Even the Australian passport control officer was keen to rub it in, saying bad luck if you are here for the cricket! We had however already heard more positive news from our pilot, that England had fared well on the first day of the Perth Test, and that left arm spinner Monty Panesar, who had finally been selected ahead of Ashley Giles, had taken 5/92, restricting Australia to 244.

Delayed in the airport in Perth because my daughter's case had not arrived with us, we arrived at our hotel with the morning papers, and I clearly remember the back page headlines leading with the words "The Fools, they should have picked Panesar earlier" (the fools being the England selectors). England's big chance evaporated quickly on the second day after Kevin Pietersen was out for 70, with England 29 runs behind on first innings, and Australia were soon back in control of the Test, closing on 119/1.

We bumped into a number of the Barmy Army fans that evening who had made their way to the Lucky Shag down on the jetty, which was the name of their designated pub for Perth, and where they met at the end of each days play, to drink and plan which songs they would sing the following day. I sent my first report back to London on the steps of the cricket museum where the famous Ashes urn was being exhibited, and then we met up for a meal with David the dentist and his family, and picked up the tickets for Saturday's play, and settled in for an early night, in anticipation of a full day's cricket tomorrow.

Emma and I had previously been to the WACA in February 1991, and on a very hot day, witnessed a poor England batting display, a day which was most notable for a fly past by a Tiger Moth plane trailing a banner which said "Gower and Morris are innocent, OK", which related to an incident earlier in the tour when the two players had taken time off from a tour game in Queensland to take a ride in a World War Two biplane. When Gower came out to bat at the WACA that day, the Aussie fans were quick to produce their inflatable airplanes, and Gower would forever be linked with what became known as the "Tiger Moth Affair".

It was perhaps fortunate that the two aviators had abandoned their plans to drop a water bomb on the ground, and whilst senior pro David Gower played the incident down, describing it as just a bit of fun, the new England Management Team comprising skipper Graham Gooch, Manager Micky Stewart and Tour Manager Peter Lush took a very dim view of proceedings and fined the pair the maximum £1,000. (In Gower's case it was £1,027 when the cost of the flight was factored in!) For both players, their international cards had now been marked, John Morris would never play again for his country, and Gower's long career which had brought so much joy to so many, would end sooner than perhaps it should have done.

Back to 2006, and as we got off the bus and started to walk around the WACA, the heat hit us, and when we found our seats, we soon discovered there was no shade at all. For the spectators, this was going to be a day for sun hats, sun cream, and lots of water, and for the players, a very tough day for the fielders, but in contrast a near perfect day for batting; and for one Australian batsman in particular, it would provide him with a career defining moment, and an unforgettable experience for those there to witness it.

There are many aspects to a cricket tour, and touring Australia is one of the toughest cricketing tours to undertake. Fitness, match preparation and form are of course key, but when you factor in the other elements including the press, the partisan crowds and the immense distances travelled, you begin to understand how difficult things can get. There is however one more element which can play a significant part in Australia, and that is the heat, and on Saturday 16th December in Perth, England went out to field at 11am with the temperature already in the 40s, and after lunch it reached 52 degrees out in the middle, and 45 degrees where we were sitting in the stand.

England's bowlers strained every sinew in the morning session, with no luck at all, and you sensed this was going to be a long day under a merciless sun for the fielding side. Hayden and Ponting and then Hussey were able to lay the platform for Australia's middle-order batsman later in the day. Mike Hussey and Michael Clarke would go on to make classy hundreds, and although Hussey quickly followed by Andrew Symonds fell to the bowling of Monty Panesar, Australia were already 365/5, with a lead approaching 400 runs. Clarke was still at the crease and closing in on his hundred and in the words of commentator Michael Slater, "he was seeing it as big as water melon now". The stage was set for some late afternoon fireworks, and boy did Adam Gilchrist explode into action.

To give you an idea how stifling the heat was, I was constantly up and down to the soft drinks stall, buying water, or orange or coke for all of us, and although we found some welcome shade in a nearby park during the lunch break, there was just no wind and no respite from the heat. I did not even think of buying a beer, which is unusual for me when watching a Test match, and not one of us needed the loo all day. About 3pm, and having given up on the Fremantle Doctor, my wife and daughter had had enough, and left early preferring the comfort of the hotel swimming pool.

It was certainly a tough day's cricket for England's beleaguered players, and it was just about to get even tougher. However, on the plus side the Barmy Army was seemingly oblivious to England's perilous situation, and despite the parched conditions, they kept up their end, and delivered their well rehearsed and very humorous song list, led by the incomparable Jimmy, ably assisted by the legendary Dave the Trumpet. Having purchased tickets through the Barmy Army, not surprisingly we were in their immediate vicinity, and they certainly kept us, and the English fans entertained, and maybe also the Australian faithful too. One character particularly stood out for me, as he was dressed in Black Tie all day, despite the heat, and it was his role to stand up when he saw fit, to then thrust out a card held in each hand, one with the word "NO", the other with the word "NONSENSE", and to bellow out the very same words to anyone who might care to listen.

Back to the cricket, and please let me explain what I mean by the Fremantle Doctor... although England's players might have needed a doctor to treat heat exhaustion and sun stroke, the "Doctor" is actually the local term given to the cooling late morning and early afternoon sea breeze which occurs in the summer in Western Australia, and blows at its strongest in the months of December and January when the temperature differential between the land and the ocean is greatest. It normally blows between 10am and 3pm, but on this day it forgot to make an appearance, until much later.

The Australian wicket-keeper, Adam Gilchrist was by all accounts in pretty poor form with the bat, and was very close to announcing his retirement before this Test. England's captain Andrew Flintoff had the wood over Gilchrist in the 2005 series, a series in which Gilchrist had only averaged 21 with the bat, against a career average of over 47 and no fewer than 16 Test centuries, which is a record for a wicket-keeper. Apparently "Gilly" was persuaded by his wife against retiring, and would emphatically put recent poor form to the back of his mind, and take full advantage of England's wilting bowling attack to score what would be his final and 17th Test century.

Gilchrist started his scoring spree with a streaky four past gully off Flintoff, and never looked back, nimbly moving his feet to the pitch of the ball and racing to an entertaining 50 off just 40 balls, his fastest ever Test 50, by taking two runs off the second ball of another Monty Panesar over. The next four balls of Monty's over went for 6, 6, 4 and 6, and suddenly Gilchrist was 73 not out, off just 44 balls, and the crowd were in a frenzy. This was certainly some of the sweetest and purest ball striking I had ever witnessed, and each six in that over just went that little bit further than the previous one. James and I were very much in the firing line at "cow corner", and so we got a birds eye view of everything, and I remember having to crane our necks to follow the trajectory of the ball.

When we had arrived at the ground, I had purchased a head set radio device, and I could now hear the commentators raising the question of what was the fastest recorded Test century ever, and we quickly found out that the record belonged to Viv Richards who had scored a 100 off just 56 balls for West Indies in Antigua in 1986. Of course Gilchrist was oblivious to this record at the time, and carried on attacking every ball. Hoggard came on for Panesar, and was immediately clobbered for six as well, as Gilchrist's score moved on to 85 off 48 balls, and Australia reached 500/5.

As we made to leave the ground, and with the benefit of ball by ball commentary in my ear, Gilchrist edged closer to his century, and still needed three off his 55th ball to break the record and then two off his 56th ball to equal the record, but Matthew Hoggard spoilt the party a bit by purposely bowling the next ball full and wide, which "Gilly" could not reach, but instead he drove the next ball for two runs to reach his 100 off 57 balls, which at the time was the second fastest Test century of all time. His second fifty had been made off just 17 balls.

This was far from being the perfect day for an England fan, but it couldn't have been much better if you were an Australian. Despite the one sided nature of the contest, we had seen some excellent batting on the day, three centuries and an explosive 6th wicket stand which had put on 162 runs in just 20 overs between Michael Clarke (135 not out) and Adam Gilchrist (102 not out).

Despite a century from Alastair Cook and 87 from Ian Bell, 51 from Flintoff, and 60 not out from Pietersen, and despite taking the game into the middle session of the fifth day, England were bowled out for 350, and lost this match by 207 runs. Australia had won the Ashes back in record time, and by the time we had arrived in Ayers Rock, and no sooner had we settled into our room, the palm device rang asking if I could take part in the Monday morning phone in back home on BBC 5 Live Radio, to which I said yes, happy to do so.

After all the euphoria of the 2005 series, and the BBC going to the lengths of running a competition for roving reporters, of which I was one, the topic of the day's phone-in back home was quite simply and starkly "why have we lost the Ashes in record time". It was only then that I was informed that I would be joining in the discussion with two rather better known cricketers and presenters, Test Match Special's Jonathan Agnew and former England captain Mike Gatting who were both live in the studio in London! When the interviewer came to me for my thoughts and observations, many of my points had already been made by the other two, but at least I was able to contribute to what was, if not a witch hunt, a fairly lively debate on England's shortcomings.

The family moved on to Adelaide next via Alice Springs and we stayed with friends over Christmas from where I was still sending reports back to the UK, and all this despite another heavy defeat in the fourth Boxing Day Test at Melbourne. We then spent New Year in Sydney where I managed to bag a free ticket to watch the first day of the final Test as well, and despite a courageous fighting 89 from skipper Flintoff, there was no stopping Australia who went on to complete a 5-0 series whitewash.

England had never recovered from the second Test final day collapse at Adelaide, and if truth be told this England side was not a patch on the one which had won in 2005. Freddie Flintoff had struggled with his own form, and with the glare of publicity away from home and the captaincy had not surprisingly become an unexpected burden. In contrast, Australia's focus to win back the Ashes in their own conditions, had been total, and this remember was one of the very best Australian teams in history. Clearly there had been no repeat of the 2005 contest, which simply goes to show that even with all the hype, in cricket, in sport, and in life generally, there are just too many variables to replicate a special series or moment in time.

Of the three main protagonists in this chapter, Andrew Flintoff would not captain England again in Test cricket, and would be plagued by an ankle injury over the next four years, but would retire on a high when he famously and theatrically ran out Australian skipper Ricky Ponting in the deciding Oval Test in the 2009 Ashes which England won 2-1. The great Ricky Ponting would never win a Test series as captain in England, despite amassing 13,378 Test runs and 41 Test centuries before his retirement in 2012. And despite Adam Gilchrist's amazing whirlwind century at the WACA, he could not fully rediscover his cricketing mojo, and retired in 2008, leaving a swashbuckling legacy for all subsequent wicket-keeper batsmen to follow.

Thankfully the cricket was just a small part of what proved to be a brilliant three week family holiday, and seeing Ayers Rock, travelling on the Ghan, spending Christmas in Adelaide and New Year's Eve on the water by the Sydney Harbour Bridge will all live long in the memory. If I could choose a profession, cricket commentator would probably be my perfect job, and when we got home a number of friends had said what a good face I had for radio! However, my biggest supporter turned out to be our local butcher in Ben Rhydding, Steve Furniss. Steve is a huge cricket fan and makes a great burger for the Barbie too, and is no stranger to early starts, which is when he said he had heard no fewer than seven of my reports on the radio.

(The cover picture for this book was taken at the WACA on 16th December 2006, and illustrates both what a beautiful day for cricket it was, and also what a fine cricketing surface the WACA was. An intimate stadium with a lightning fast outfield and a 20,000 seat capacity, England played their last Test match there in 2017, and the Western Australian Cricket Association officially moved to the brand new 60,000 seater multi-sports "Perth Stadium" in January 2018, also known as the Optus Stadium, which is located just across the River Swan in the neighbouring suburb of Burswood).

Chapter 13
I wish I was an Olympian

London 2012 Olympics:
Mens Olympic Hockey Final: Saturday 11th August

Britain's Roger Bannister ran the first ever sub 4 minute mile at the Iffley Road Track in Oxford, in a time of 3 minutes 59.4 seconds, on May 6th 1954, and I remember my father telling me exactly where he was when it happened, and that he was making his way to evening cricket practice, cricket bag in one hand, transistor radio in the other pressed to his ear, listening intently to the BBC broadcast which was commentated by the 1924 Olympic 100 metres champion, Harold Abrahams, of Chariots of Fire fame.

And 51 years later on July 6th 2005, I was driving through Rotherham of all places when the IOC President Jacques Rogge said the simple words: "The 2012 Games are awarded to the City of London". I was on my own in the car at the time but screamed with delight at the news and fist pumped the air and also blew the car horn for good effect. No doubt anyone watching my erratic behavior would have phoned the police, but at the time, I was certainly of the same opinion as our Prime Minister Tony Blair, who described it "as a momentous day for Britain".

Ever since I collected a petrol station sticker book about the Olympic Games I have been fascinated by them, and I had always wanted to see the action live at some stage. I was hoping that would be in Greece in 1996, but for some reason, the IOC disregarded sentiment, preferring to follow the dollar and awarded the Games instead to Atlanta, which just happened to be the head office of a global drinks corporation called Coca-Cola. I was delighted to see that Athens was finally awarded the 2004 games, and when it was announced the games were coming to London, I knew then that this would be my big chance to be there in person.

My first recollections of the Olympics are vague, but I remember getting up early in the morning and watching black and white images on the TV as well as seeing hurdler David Hemery winning a gold medal, so that means I was watching the 1968 Mexico Games. A personal interest in track and field soon followed, as I soon realised I was quick, and the summer inter-house athletics events were the ideal platform for me to progress. The school also had a fairly basic outdoor long jump pit as well as an indoor high-jump area, replete with a good pile of old mattresses as our landing area, and I recall spending hours trying to perfect my scissors jump, and also the more daring Fosbury Flop, named after the American high jumper Dick Fosbury, who won a gold medal at the 1968 Olympics.

School athletics often got in the way of the cricket season, but there was always time for Standards at the start of the summer term. Standards was a great concept, because it was something everyone was encouraged to try out, and you could enter as many events as you wanted, but only your best four standards would count, and you had to include at least one track and one field event.

Four "A" standards were worth three points each, so an individual could get a maximum of 12 points. The event was open to everyone, and every year group, and your house competed against other houses for the Standards Cup, so it was a case of encouraging everyone to take part, because the points were added together to see which house won overall. Preferring the sprint events, I did have a go at all the field events too, including the shot, javelin, discus, triple jump and long jump. I remember the discus on a wet day being one of the most dangerous spectator sports possible!

Of all the events, and based on one huge long jump which I was never able to replicate, I have always enjoyed this event more than any other, so it was my goal to try and obtain tickets for the evening of the Mens Long Jump Final which was set to take place on Saturday 4th August 2012. There was a big scramble for tickets, and perhaps not surprisingly they were oversubscribed, (which meant the family would miss out on Super Saturday as it became known), and I was also unlucky with the ballot on other days, so the prospect of not being able to get a ticket for any day was suddenly a distinct reality.

However, in the weeks leading up to the Games, I was walking past our local Thomas Cook travel agent and noticed they were offering Olympic packages in the shop window. I went straight in to enquire and impulsively purchased the package which comprised two tickets to the Women's Volleyball Bronze Medal match, and two tickets to the Mens Hockey Final, both events taking place on Saturday 11th August, the penultimate day of the games. Also included in the package was a two night stay in a central hotel near Marble Arch.

The BBC coverage of the 2012 Olympics was excellent from start to finish. The opening ceremony was spectacularly British, and culminated in the lighting of the Olympic flame, which was delivered to the stadium by speedboat and the ubiquitous David Beckham, who handed it on to five times Olympic Gold Medal winner Sir Steve Redgrave, who in turn handed it on to seven specially chosen young athletes of the future. The nation was gripped, and our athletes were inspired to great deeds, and our medal tally just kept on rising day by day, with the daily highlights being introduced by Gabby Logan and medals won on that day being individually acclaimed to the strains of Spandau Ballet's "GOLD".

Great Britain had its best ever Games, finishing third overall in the medal table with a total of 65 medals including 29 Gold, (in 17 different sports), 17 Silver and 19 Bronze. Super Saturday on 4th August proved to be the nation's single most productive medal day since 1908, when no fewer than six Gold medals were won, starting with Rowing and the Men's Coxless four, and the Women's lightweight double sculls, then the Women's team pursuit in cycling, and then three further golds in the Athletics stadium in the evening.

We watched all the action at home through the day, and then tuned in again for the Athletics about 8pm, and what an atmosphere there was in the stadium, and what a treat we were in for when firstly our poster girl for the games, Sheffield's Jess Ennis-Hill, finished her 800 metres to win Heptathlon Gold, quickly followed by Bletchley's Greg Rutherford and his Gold in the Long Jump after leaping 8 metres 31 in the fourth round, and to round things off, our third Gold in just 45 minutes was secured by Somalian born Londoner, Mo Farah, in the 10,000 metres.

Communities across the UK had engaged with the Olympic Torch relays in the build up to the Games, and thousands were inspired to get involved and either volunteered to be Games Makers, or purchased tickets to see the action at any one of the many great venues around London from Horse Guards Parade for the beach volleyball, to Lords for the archery, to the Olympic Stadium for the athletics. Quite clearly our athletes were also inspired by their surroundings and excelled.

After Super Saturday, my son and I had a full week to wait before we would get our chance to get our Olympic fix, and I remember anticipation was high when we finally boarded the afternoon train down to Kings Cross on Friday 10th August. We found our hotel easily enough, unpacked, and realising that the biggest Fan Zone was just over the road in Hyde Park, we made our way there, picnicked outside with hundreds of others in the sunshine, before the park opened for the evening's events.

There was another packed athletics programme in the

Olympic Stadium to enjoy, and also the bronze medal women's hockey match, which Great Britain won 3-1 against New Zealand, and then later the final, which we watched on one of the Fan Zone's many huge screens with a crowd of excitable Dutch supporters, who saw their women beat Argentina 2-0 to take gold. There were food outlets and bars everywhere, once again the organisation was excellent, and the pervading friendly and cosmopolitan atmosphere was infectious.

Saturday dawned, and after a good hearty breakfast, we made our way by tube to Earl's Court, which was the venue for the indoor volleyball. The transport links and directional signs were also excellent, and the military were on hand to help facilitate speedy security checks, and as a result we were quickly in our seats a good hour before the start of the match. James and I had no previous knowledge of volleyball, but in the build up the announcer made sure the uninitiated understood all the terms, so that we could tell our sets from our digs, and our blocks from our spikes, and we also had a turn to virtually play the bongo drums!

Great Britain's women's volleyball team had played in the preliminary round and had notched up a win against lowly Algeria 3-2, but had not made it through to the knock-out stages, which had been dominated by Brazil and the United States, who would play each other in the final, which Brazil went on to win 3-1. We got to see the Bronze Medal match, along with about 10,000 other spectators, which Japan won by three sets to nil, against South Korea, winning three close sets (25-22, 26-24 and 25-21). This had been our appetiser, and now we were heading for Olympic Park itself.

Again, London's transport links were outstanding, and remarkably it took less than hour to get across London from Earl's Court to Westfield Stratford City via tube and javelin train. We made our way through the shopping centre and just followed the signs all the way to the Olympic Park, where the Games Makers were immediately friendly and pointed us in the right direction, and we were in the park and free to roam around, grab a bite to eat, and watch the action on any of a number of large screens which included the Men's Bronze medal hockey match at Park Live, which Great Britain lost 3-1 to Australia. We met up with a number of friends from Ben Rhydding Hockey Club for beers, before our main event, the Men's Hockey Final at 8pm.

The purpose built hockey stadium had a capacity of 15,000, and it was full of Dutch, German and neutral supporters, and the more colourfully dressed Dutch supporters were in loud voice, and gloriously accompanied by their very own brass band, and certainly made all the early noise and added to the party atmosphere. The Germans seemed happy to soak up pressure in the first half, and whilst the Dutch played the better hockey, chances were few and far between, so it came as a bit of a surprise when Germany's winger Jan-Philipp Rabente cut in from the right, skillfully shrugged off two tackles and deftly tucked the ball past the keeper just inside the left hand post, to give Germany the lead just before half-time.

The Germans started the stronger in the second half and hit the post after about ten minutes, but the Dutch fought back into the game, forcing a number of short corners, from one of which Mink van der Weerden equalized to set up an exciting last fifteen minutes. With about five minutes remaining Germany took a quick hit and caught the Dutch napping, and in ghosted that man Rabente again, taking up an unmarked position just outside the right hand post, and deflecting home the winning goal. Two bits of individual brilliance from Rabente in a very tight game was the only difference between the two teams, and Germany had retained its Olympic Hockey title.

What a lengthy medal ceremony followed next! Australia who had beaten GB earlier in the day were up first to get their Bronze medals, then the Dutch to get their Silvers, and then the Germans to get their Gold Medals. All in all, 49 medals, 49 sets of flowers, and then finally the German national anthem. We then left the hockey stadium, and made our way back towards the exits, and congregated under the BBC tower, which was actually a series of colourful containers irregularly placed one on top of each, with a balcony at the top. We had heard rumours that Mo Farah would be making an appearance, having done the double by winning the 5,000 metres earlier in the evening, so we hung around to see what would happen, and behind us a big expectant crowd continued to gather.

An 18 year old Tom Daley had also won Bronze in the 10 metre platform event during the hockey final, but the crowd were getting restless, and we all started singing "We Want Mo", to which Gabby Logan then appeared above us looking like an angel dressed in white, promising us a surprise, but only after the news and lottery had finished. For good measure, and true to her word, Gabby did reappear, but not on her own, firstly with David Beckham, then Katherine Grainger, then Michael Johnson and then Ben Ainslie, all to great cheers.

We left the park at about 11pm, merging with hundreds of others from all sorts of nations, including a large group of delighted Norwegians with cowbells who were celebrating a Women's handball gold medal. Everyone was in high spirits, enjoying the moment, thanking the Games Makers who were still happy to help direct us back to the station. We soaked up every last drop of atmosphere that we could, both wallowing in the glow of a very special day at a very special event, at London 2012.

In this fast paced materialistic world of ours, more than ever we need the constancy of a globally inclusive event, and there is no bigger or better example of this than the Olympic Games. In the modern era, only world war or pandemic has cancelled the four yearly ritual of the Games, and it remains the pinnacle of achievement for any athlete. The words spoken by the founder of the modern Olympic movement, Baron Pierre de Coubertin, still ring true... "The important thing in the Olympic Games is not winning but taking part; the essential thing in life is not conquering but fighting well".

I am pretty sure that I will not live to see another home Games, so I am therefore delighted to say that I managed to play a very small supporting part at London 2012 with my son. We thoroughly enjoyed the unique experience and atmosphere, and my advice if you are not good enough as an athlete to compete in the Games, would be instead to make a mental note to add the Olympics to your proverbial bucket list, whether it be in Tokyo which we hope will take place in 2021 now, or Los Angeles in 2024, or Paris in 2028, or beyond these confirmed dates, and as and when future venues are announced.

A postscript to this Olympic chapter, relates to legacy. Creating a permanent hockey legacy was one of the many pledges in London's Olympic bid, and the opening of the Lee Valley Hockey Centre delivered on this promise for both elite and club players, and this story has a happy ending for those like myself who are connected to one of Yorkshire's oldest and most prestigious clubs, Ben Rhydding Hockey Club.

Our Men's Masters (over 50s) have enjoyed great success in recent years, culminating in three national finals in four years, and winning in 2014 and 2016. What a game we had in 2016 against Richmond at the Olympic Park venue, creating our own slice of history, as we came back from 2-0 down, in a breathless game that was characterised by countless injuries and substitutions, five green and six yellow cards, at the end of which Ben Rhydding edged a seven goal thriller to win 4-3.

And at the elite level of the sport, Great Britain's Women went on to win Gold at the 2016 Olympic Hockey final against the Netherlands. Having drawn an exciting game 3-3 in normal time, GB goalkeeper Maddie Hinch remarkably kept a clean sheet in a thrilling penalty shuttle shoot out - now that would have been an amazing match to witness!

Chapter 14
Taking Root

2nd Ashes Test – Lords – July 20th 2013

I have been fortunate to visit some of the most iconic cricket grounds around the world including the MCG, the Adelaide Oval, the WACA and the SCG in Australia, Kensington Oval in Barbados, and Edgbaston, Old Trafford, Headingley and the Oval here in England. Hopefully in the not too distant future I will be able to add perhaps the most picturesque ground of all, Newlands, nestled under Table Mountain in Cape Town to the list. All of the above grounds have their very own tradition, history and atmosphere, but there is one venue which in my view stands head and shoulders above all the others, and that is the very home of cricket, Lords Cricket Ground, St John's Wood, London NW8.

I have visited Lords on a number of occasions, and the first time was memorable in as much as my father took me as a 12 year old boy to watch the first day of the 2nd Ashes Test on 31st July 1975. I say memorable, but only because it gets a diary entry, which simply summarises the day's play as follows: "Saw the Queen, England made 313/9, and captain Tony Greig top scored with 96". Other than that, I only have vague memories of being very impressed with the Australian opening bowling attack of Dennis Lillee and Jeff Thompson who were very quick and intimidating, and took a number of quick wickets, and only the bespectacled and diminutive and grey haired David Steele stood firm. England's John Edrich made 175 in the second innings, but the game ended in a high scoring but ultimately uneventful draw.

At the time I guess I was too young to understand the importance of the Ashes, or indeed to fully appreciate my surroundings, but this began to change when the following year I was fortunate to be enrolled onto a cricket coaching course run by one of Yorkshire's finest spin bowlers, Don Wilson, who also happened to be the incumbent coach at the Indoor Cricket School at Lords, as well as our school cricket coach. The course ran for three days, and I benefitted hugely from the experience and the quality of coaching, and to add to the thrill of the big city, each morning I was driven to Lords by my older sister's boss, who just happened to be "Wish You Were Here's" Judith Chalmers.

Moving forward to 2008, I organised another memorable outing to Lords for eight members of my family, which started in Northampton, from where we were taxied in a big white limousine by a West Indian chauffeur who had the distinct look of the crocodile farm handler with a hooked hand in the Bond Film, Live and Let Die. In reality, he was an absolute gentleman, called Larry, who calmly navigated all the traffic and dropped us off at the iconic Grace Gates, so this was door to door service with style, and many a head turned to see just which celebrities were alighting from his shining white stretch limo.

We were there for the second day of the 1st Test v South Africa, and despite a bit of rain, we saw Kevin Pietersen improve his overnight score of 104 to 152, and Ian Bell improve his from 75 to 199, only to be expertly caught by the bowler Paul Harris as he pressed for his double century. England enjoyed an excellent batting day, eventually declaring on a mammoth 593/8, but once again the match would peter out into a high scoring and tame draw.

Either of the above two visits to Lords might for different reasons have earned their own chapter in this book, but both were beaten into second equal by a very special day and Ashes triumph at Lords on Saturday 20th July 2013. Special, because this was a 50th birthday present from a very good friend, we had the best seats in the house, the company and the atmosphere was spot on, and it was the perfect day for England and Yorkshire, and it ultimately led to a very rare win at Lords for England against the old enemy.

Scoring a Test match hundred, or taking a five wicket haul in an innings or 10 or more wickets in a match at the home of cricket must be a very proud moment, especially as it results in the successful player having his or her achievement marked on one of Lords' Honours Boards which are situated in the home and away dressing rooms. The Honours Boards are one of Lords' many endearing traditions and what an accolade it must be to have your name inscribed for your peers to see.

Sir Ian Botham, who received the members silent treatment all those years ago in 1981, holds the record for the most appearances on the boards with ten; eight five-wicket innings, one ten-wicket match and one century. Conversely many great players are not named on the boards, and these include England's Mike Atherton who came agonisingly close only to be run out on 99 going for his third run, Shane Warne, Brian Lara, Curtly Ambrose, and perhaps most surprisingly Sachin Tendulkar.

If there is a down side to the Honours Boards, then I suppose it is that every visiting player also wants to do well at Lords, which might account for the fact that this ground has all too often been a happy hunting ground for visiting teams, particularly Australian sides.

Australian players perhaps have an even greater edge than other nations do, given the importance and enduring nature of the Ashes contest, which is cricket's oldest match up. The first Ashes Test at Lords took place in 1884, and prior to the 2013 series, there had been 34 Tests played, of which England had only won six, Australia 14, with another 14 matches being drawn. The Australians evidently enjoy making their mark at Lords!

Remarkably you had to go back to 1934 to register a home victory, and this was achieved largely by the hand of one man, Yorkshire and England's Hedley Verity who took a record fourteen wickets in one day, including the great Donald Bradman in both innings, on his way to producing the best ever Test match bowling figures by an Englishman at Lords of 15/104. Bradman's assessment of Verity ranks with any. "With Hedley, I am never quite sure. You see, there's no breaking point with him". Remarkably, this would be England's only Ashes victory at Lords in the 20th century, and perhaps even more remarkably, Verity's wicket haul would be surpassed by Australian Bob Massie who on debut took 16/137 in the Lords Test of 1972.

Australia's only victory in that incredible 2005 Ashes series not surprisingly came at Lords too. However, under Andrew Strauss' captaincy in 2009, England finally broke their 75 year wait, and beat Australia by 115 runs. Strauss scored a brilliant 161 in England's first innings, putting on 196 for the first wicket with Alastair Cook, and despite a fine second innings 136 from Michael Clarke, Freddie Flintoff sealed the long awaited victory with 5/92.

FEC is an often used abbreviation in English cricket, and stands for Future England Captain. This was certainly a term levelled at Alastair Cook, and sure enough on the retirement of Andrew Strauss in 2012, Cook took over as England's captain, which meant his first Ashes series would be the 2013 home series, and another FEC, Yorkshireman Joe Root, would play the dominant innings which would buck the trend and secure back to back Ashes Test victories at Lords.

However, please let me set the scene for you. There were four of us making our way to Lords early that Saturday morning. Three of us, Richard, Sam and myself had travelled from Yorkshire on the 7am train out of Leeds, which arrived about 9.30am at Kings Cross, allowing us ample time to take the tube to St John's Wood, where we would meet our organiser Alex outside the ground. Alex had himself taken the train from Newbury, having been at a stag party the day before. All present and correct, we merged with the well natured throng of expectant spectators, and made our way up to our seats at the top of the Mound Stand, close to the bar and dining area, with a great side-on view of the ground, the iconic twin towered members and players pavilion to our left, and the impressive and futuristic media centre to our right, the famous Lords slope clearly visible. Perhaps most importantly the weather was set fair so we knew we were in for a full day's cricket.

We also knew that the match situation had shifted significantly in favour of England after a great second day for the home team. England had made 361 all out in their first innings, Ian Bell top scoring with 109, then Jonny Bairstow with 67. In reply, Australia were dismissed for just 128 in their first innings, thanks largely to some excellent bowling by off-spinner Graeme Swann who took 5/44.

Everyone needs a bit of luck, and Swann certainly got it with his first wicket, which was a bizarre dismissal, a big loopy long hop of a full toss, described by some as the worst ball ever to take a wicket, which Chris Rogers simply missed when trying to pull it for six, and hitting the pads, the England team went up in unison, and almost in shock and surprise, umpire Erasmus had no hesitation in raising his finger. However, if Rogers has reviewed the decision, he would have been reprieved as it was missing the stumps by some margin. Australia had been 50/1 at that point, and seemingly in control, but would then collapse, losing their final nine wickets for just 78 runs in the space of 53 overs.

England finished the second day in a bit of second innings bother themselves on 31/3, with Joe Root, who had opened the innings, still there on 18 not out, and night watchman Tim Bresnan 0 not out. Australia were indebted to Peter Siddle who had given his team hope of salvation by taking all three wickets to fall, these being the three prize scalps of Alistair Cook, Jonathan Trott and Kevin Pietersen.

Most spectators were in their seats by 10.45am, eager to see the first ball, and not wanting to miss any of the action. Yes, England were well ahead of the game, but needed a good start to drive home their advantage, and as soon as play got underway, there was a distinct audible murmur of hushed conversations emanating from all parts of the ground, a happy and expectant hum that would prevail throughout the day.

The morning's play was gripping in the traditional sense, in that neither batsman was prepared to take any risks, and the bowling was tight, so only 83 runs were scored in the session. Joe Root had reached his fifty, but crucially England had not lost any wickets, and were now in full command of the match. Lunch was a wonderfully relaxed interruption, waiter service, a delicious three course meal with perfectly chilled white wine, and some great company and conversation. We took our time, and enjoyed a long lunch, and when play restarted 40 minutes later, we did not miss any of the cricket because we still had a good view of proceedings from our lofty table.

Tim Bresnan went soon after lunch for a very patient 38 off

137 balls, and made way for the first innings centurion Ian Bell. The pace of scoring was similar to the first session, and when the tea-break arrived at 3.40pm, England had advanced to 171/4, which meant the lead was already 404 runs. Root was tantalisingly still three runs short of his hundred. There then followed a quick and quintessentially English tea of sandwiches, scones and cakes, and more wine, but this time when the players came back out, and with Root just one shot away from his 100, we returned to our seats in expectation to wish Joe to his milestone.

The Lords crowd is so knowledgeable. Many are regulars who take the same seat on the same corresponding day every year, and have therefore forged great friendships over time, watching cricket at Lords. Many are there for a special occasion, as we were, but this does not stop the good mannered banter between strangers, and you do meet some incredible people. Alex was sat next to a very well dressed couple who offered him a glass of wine, which he enjoyed, and complimenting the couple on their good taste, he was then informed that the wine was from their own vineyard, and that they had flown in for the day from Geneva. As a parting shot at the end of the day, they gifted Alex two bottles of wine!

Back to the action, and Root took his time and moved up to 99 not out with two singles, and then the right ball came along, a little short and wide, and he square cut Ashton Agar for four to bring up his century, his first century at Lords, his second Test century, and his first Ashes hundred. The crowd had been waiting patiently for this moment, and we were all quickly to our feet once we saw that the ball had pierced the infield, and was racing away over the quick outfield. Root's fresh faced smile said it all, arms aloft, bat in one hand, helmet in the other, and at that moment we knew, as did all the cricketing world, that Joe Root's career had been well and truly launched. A new name for the home dressing room Honours Board, and what a sense of occasion the young smiling Yorkshireman had, a first Ashes century on a glorious Saturday at Lords!

Root and Bell now went through the gears, and boundaries began to flow, as did the wine and beer, in the glorious afternoon sunshine. The pair added 151 for the fifth wicket, before Ian Bell was out for 74. Bell's dismissal brought another Yorkshireman to the crease, Jonny Bairstow. Root then passed 150, and was now in full flow, and England closed the day on 333/5, with Root, having batted all day, 178 not out, and Bairstow 11 not out. If the scoring rate in the first two sessions had been slow, England made up for it by scoring 162 runs in the evening session at over five runs per over, leaving Australia 566 in arrears.

A perfect day to be at the home of cricket to witness a great day for England, and for Joe Root, and all four of us made it back to Ilkley that evening, and there was still time and energy for a celebratory drink! England wrapped up victory the following day, bowling Australia out for 235, and winning the match by a mammoth 347 runs. Graeme Swann once again starred with the ball and took four more wickets to give him match figures of 9/122, but Joe Root was named Man of the Match. England went 2-0 up in the series, a series they would go on to win 3-0.

Joe Root inherited the title FEC, and became England's 80th Test captain when Alastair Cook resigned the position in 2017. To date Joe has scored 17 Test centuries, three of which have been at Lords. It's clearly a ground he likes batting on having scored 180 v Australia, 190 against South Africa, and 200 not out against Sri Lanka. He has also scored 16 ODI centuries, including 113 not out against India at Lords, and in the summer of 2019, he was England's top scorer in the World Cup, and experienced victory against New Zealand in that nerve jangling final which went to a super over, at Lords.

What's the best thing about Lords? For want of a better description, I will call it the "Lords Buzz". You can hear it in the ground, and if you are listening to TMS, you can hear it as a constant in the background behind the voices of the commentators. It's the product of a knowledgeable and respectful crowd, who love their cricket, and it's the sound of relaxed mutterings, which creates its own unique atmosphere. Lords is the home of cricket for a reason, where everything runs smoothly without fuss, where manners and politeness are always on show. It's the temple of cricket, designed and moulded by the disciples of the game, in perpetuity.

Chapter 15
The Home of Golf

The Old Course, St Andrews
The 144th Open Championship: July 18th-20th 2015

It is thought that golf in St Andrews dates back to the early 15th century, and we know it was a popular pastime because King James II of Scotland banned the game of golf in 1457 because he felt that young men were playing too much golf instead of practising archery. King James III upheld the ban too, and it was only when keen golfer King James IV came to the throne in 1502 that the ban was lifted. Then in 1552, Archbishop John Hamilton granted the people of St Andrews the right to play golf on the links land, and two centuries later in 1754, twenty-two noblemen, landowners and professors founded the Society of St Andrews, the precursor to what we now know as the Royal and Ancient Golf Club.

The Royal and Ancient Golf Club of St Andrews is therefore acknowledged across the world as the home of golf, and its most famous golf course, the Old Course, is not only the most regularly used course on the Open rota, but according to the most successful golfer of all time, Jack Nicklaus, "if you're going to be a player people will remember, you have to win the Open at St Andrews". Nicklaus was one of just a handful of golfers who over the years won two Opens at the Old Course, and also said in 2005 "I'm very sentimental and the place gets me every time I go there. St Andrews was always where I wanted to finish my major career".

Bobby Jones is another who fell in love with the Old Course. Jones first played there in the 1921 Championship, and famously could not get out of the bunker on the 11th hole, lost his temper, and did not complete his card, thereby disqualifying himself. However six years later he was back to win the Open wire to wire by six clear shots, and returned in 1930 to win the British Amateur, on his way to winning the other three majors in that year, making him the only man in the history of golf to win the Grand Slam. Jones went on to fall in love with the Old Course for the rest of his life and in 1958 he was awarded the key to the city and said "I could take out of my life everything but my experiences here in St Andrews and I would still have had a rich and full life".

Evidently there is something very special about the links land in this part of Scotland, and the Old Course can make even the best professional and amateur golfers in the world quake in their boots. I can assure you that for less capable golfers like myself, trembling knees and heart palpitations are also very much the order of the day, as I was to experience in April 2010, when I was lucky enough to play the Old Course, the New Course and the Castle Course, three of the seven courses that are now managed by the St Andrews Links Trust.

The Old Course is a public course on common land and is held in trust by the St Andrews Links Trust by an act of Parliament, so remarkably it is open to non-members as well as members, and so long as you have an official handicap certificate, there are a number of ways that the public might get a tee time to play the oldest and most famous golf course in the world. The best way to guarantee a tee-time is to write to the Trust in the autumn when group booking requests are accepted. Then, if your party is prepared to book well in advance, and take the shoulder season, the price can be very reasonable when compared to other championship courses, none of which can boast the heritage of St Andrews.

St Andrews, also affectionately known as "The Auld Grey Toon" due to the granite colour of many of its buildings, is situated about 30 miles north east of Edinburgh, and 10 miles south of Dundee, and has been a university town since the early 14th century, making it Scotland's oldest university. The moment you arrive in St Andrews, you are taken in by the tradition and intimacy of the town, with the Old Course Hotel prominent on your left as a golfing landmark, the relatively small town which is home to about 15,000 people then reveals itself as you drive along Main Street, and it is therefore easy to get your bearings quickly.

Our guest house slept ten people and was centrally located on Main Street, and was clearly a regular stop for golfing parties, because not only was there a small putting green in the back garden, there were also ten golf bag slots in the hall-way. Once the car has been parked, there is little need to use it again, and it is a very common sight to see golfers dressed for action, golf bags strapped to their backs, making their way down to the area of the town dominated by the impressive and iconic Royal and Ancient Clubhouse, which marks the start and finish point of the Old Course, and from where the links land stretches out as far as the eye can see.

It is easy to remember the exact date of our trip for two reasons. The first was that it coincided with the Ash Cloud which had emanated from that impossible to spell or pronounce volcano in Iceland called Eyjafjallajokull. And secondly, and when we made our way down to the Old Course for the first time, workmen were busy erecting the stands for that summers Open, in mid-April 2010.

We played the New Course first and not only did this give us the opportunity to warm up before we tackled the Old Course the following day, it also gave us a feel for the turf, and as it had various touch points with the Old Course, we got a flavour of what laid in wait for us. Built in 1895, the New Course is thus called because it was the second course to be built after the Old Course. It is an excellent golf course in its own right, and provided us all with a stiff test, which was exactly what was needed. Despite the ash cloud, and apart from the resulting dry throat which we all seemed to contract, and which became less dry once we found the bars of an evening, we were blessed with bright blue skies, and played in shirt sleeves for most of the weekend.

All eight golfers were up nice and early the following morning, a hearty breakfast, and we set off on foot in eager anticipation and no little trepidation to play the Old Course.

Pairings and teams had been drawn the day before, and most of us had not played the course before, so we purchased the services of two caddies for our fourball, which we deemed to be the done thing, partly because we wanted to enhance our Old Course experience to the full, and partly because we were told that it would help us enormously to have a "guide" to help us plot our way around the unusual layout, as well as help with our yardages and club selections.

The vista that awaits you on the first tee at the Old Course is incredible. Straight ahead is one of the widest expanses of fairway you can imagine, as it is a shared fairway for the 1st and 18th holes, and to the right the spectator stands were being erected. To the left is the iconic 18th green, fronted by the "Valley of Sin" and the white fence which marks the right hand edge of the 18th fairway, and the narrow Links Road which runs in front of the row of iconic buildings which include Tom Morris' Golf Shop (which itself backs onto another famous golf shop, Auchterlonies of St Andrews), Rusacks Hotel, and the St Andrews Golf Club.

The land is completely flat, and there are no bunkers in sight, but you can also make out the Swilcan Bridge, and the line of the Swilcan Burn which only comes into play for your second shot, and runs across the fairway and five yards in front of the green. If the surroundings on their own were enough to make your knees tremble, the wait to watch all seven golfers tee-off before me and hit good drives was further reason to be anxious, and to cap it all we were all individually announced onto the tee by the friendly official starter. I have never been more nervous on a golf course, but nerves make you concentrate, and thankfully I too hit a good drive.

I also hit a lovely second shot to the centre of the green having taken an extra club on the advice of my caddie, so there was some confusion when I got to my ball and found it about six yards short of the burn, which left me a terrifyingly delicate chip to a front flag over the infamous Swilcan burn. I was too strong with my chip, and three putted for a double bogey, but thankfully my partner made par, and I was on my way, and now able to relax a little!

Not that the course got any easier, but with the help of our caddie we at least had good advice as to where to aim, and most importantly he knew where all the bunkers were. St Andrews has 112 bunkers in total, and all are named, like the Principal's Nose or Spectacles, and some more ominously like the Coffins on the 13th hole, Hell Bunker on the 14th and the dreaded Road Hole bunker at the 17th hole. Then there is the enormous Shell bunker on the 7th, and the hugely demanding short 11th hole is also well protected by Hill and Strath bunkers. Avoid the bunkers and you will be able to keep your score going, as Bobby Jones had found out all those years ago.

The layout of the course is so different too. There are only four single greens, these being the 1st, the 9th, the 17th and the 18th. This means that there are seven double greens, which are unique in size and shape, and just enormous putting surfaces, each with two flags, and it is not unusual to find yourself with a putt of 60 feet or more, and when you factor in the close cut nature of the greens, which makes them unusually quick, almost like putting on glass, you realise that even with the deftest of touches, there are no tap ins on the Old Course.

The 14th hole is simply called "Long", and is not surprisingly the longest hole on the course. It is also a very difficult hole to picture if you are playing the course for the first time, and according to the course planner, and in terms of sticking to a strategy, it is a model golf hole the world over. The planner also provides the somewhat unhelpful notes from the great Bobby Jones: "in four rounds I am certain that depending upon the wind, I took three entirely different routes to the hole".

In our very close contest, I recall avoiding the bunkers called the Beardies off the tee, finding instead the relative calm of the fairway, delightfully named the Elysian Fields, from where I fortunately pulled my second shot to the left of the vast and dreaded trap, known as Hell Bunker, which allowed me sight of the green and flagstick for the first time on the hole. My third shot was quite promising but rolled off the putting surface, which left me something in the region of an 80 foot putt which I left about five foot from the pin, and holed for a memorable and very hard earned par which was still only good enough to halve the hole. My regulation par four at the 16th was made with far less fuss, but was good enough to win the hole.

The Road Hole was quite a challenge too. Firstly you are faced with a daunting drive, because you need to drive over the left edge of the Old Course Hotel which means you must carry out of bounds to reach the fairway. To help with your aim, the "Old Course Hotel" is spelled out for you in huge letters, and a brave golfer will aim over the word "Hotel", and a nervous golfer will aim over the word "Old". I went down the middle but hooked the ball into the rough on the left, from where I found a decent lie and hit a great fairway wood to the right hand edge of the green, avoiding that infamous bunker where Tommy Nakajima once took seven shots, and avoiding the wall and road behind the green which cost Tom Watson the 1984 Open. After a neat chip, I took two putts and proudly walked off the green having made a bogey five.

The 18th hole is an incredible sight to behold, and with our match poised all square, the nerves were twitching yet again. You cannot help but think of all the greats who have played the game, and just seeing the Swilcan Bridge in front of you and the Royal and Ancient Clubhouse in the distance standing with club in hand on the tee is an experience all on its own. You let your imagination run wild, and pretend that all you need is a par four to win your version of the Open. A good drive helped, and a slightly pushed second which carried the Valley of Sin, but also flirted with the out of bounds fence on the right, left me with a long curling right to left putt, which resulted in an inevitable three putt, but we finished our match all square, which seemed a fitting climax to our amazing adventure on the Old Course.

To complete our visit to the spiritual home of golf, we played a third golf course on the Friday, and once again we were blessed with great weather. Having enjoyed the New and the Old Courses, our three round bargain package included soup and sandwich lunches on the first 2 days, and a £28 supplement to play the youngest course, The Castle Course, which was built in 2008 on a dramatic cliff-top location south of St Andrews, affording amazing views of the Auld Grey Toon and St Andrews Bay and the North Sea beyond it – and all for £198/person. Perhaps most spectacular were the short 17th, and the par five 18th holes, which hugged the shoreline and demanded extreme concentration. On tour, we always play a game within a game, that the last player to lose his original ball from the first round scoops a £40 pot; well somehow I managed to play all three rounds with my original ball, but the prize was shared, because so did my playing partner James.

The Open Championship played later in the year in July resulted in a runaway seven shot victory and a first major title for South Africa's Louis Oosthuizen, who on a tranquil first day carded a seven under par 65 to lie in second place two shots behind Northern Ireland's rising twenty year old star, Rory McIlroy, who had set a blistering pace with a nine under par round of 63. Conditions favoured the early starters in the second round, and Oosthuizen made the most of the luck of the draw by posting a 67 to move to 12 under. McIlroy was caught up in the afternoon gales and could only shoot 80. Oosthuizen had opened up a five shot lead, and never looked back, cruising to victory with final rounds of 69 and 71 for a sixteen under total of 272, Lee Westwood finishing second, and McIlroy in a tie for third.

The 144th Open Championship returned to St Andrews in July 2015, and disappointingly saw the withdrawal of World Number 1 and current Open Champion Rory McIlroy before a ball had been hit due to an unfortunate ankle injury.

However, the current Masters and US Open Champion Jordan Spieth was in the field, and was attempting to win a third consecutive major title, and both he and the 2010 champion, Louis Oosthuizen, would find themselves very much in the mix on a final round which would be played out on a Monday for only the second time in Open history due to heavy rain and strong winds which brought about two enforced suspensions of play on Friday and Saturday.

A very good friend was working all week at the Open, as John Daly's agent, and he kindly suggested I accompany him up to St Andrews on the Saturday. The colourful John Daly had stunned the golfing world by winning the 1995 Open at St Andrews, with an outstanding display of long hitting and wonderful putting, particularly from long distance, and he clearly still has a very strong affinity with the Old Course, as evidenced by an opening round of 66 in the 2010 championship. Despite getting on in years, there he was again in 2015, drawing in the crowds, in his trademark garish garb, this time light green and pink, he was making a first round charge to reach four under par after 10 holes, before frittering shots away, which would disappointingly end in a missed cut by one single shot.

Our plan was to watch as much golf as we could on Saturday, stay overnight, and then watch the final round, and drive home on Sunday night. With the promise of free entry and passes into some of the player only areas, I jumped at the chance, and because of the high winds which brought a long delay to proceedings on Saturday, we took our time driving up, enjoyed a stop at the wonderful Gleneagles, before catching two hours of play at the end of a very curtailed day's golf. As some players still had to complete their second rounds, the decision to extend the tournament into an extra day was made there and then, and as a result we decided to stay the extra night as well, which would allow us to watch the final round on Monday.

As second round leader Dustin Johnson fell away, Australia's Mark Leishman made the biggest move with a brilliant 64, and Jordan Spieth's 66 moved him up into fourth place, one shot behind three joint leaders on 12 under par, another Australian, Jason Day, the 2010 champion, Louis Oosthuizen, and the surprise package of the day, amateur Paul Dunne from Ireland, who became the first amateur to lead the Open into the final round since Bobby Jones in 1927. Padraig Harrington, the 2007 and 2008 champion was in fifth place after a fine 65, and there were no fewer than nine players tied on nine under par, so with fourteen players within three shots of the lead, the wind and rain ravaged tournament was now set up beautifully for a thrilling finish.

After the third round had finished, we decided to have a bite to eat in the players pavilion, which to amateur golfers is better known as the Links Clubhouse which serves the Old, New and Jubilee courses. It was quite late in the day and there were only four players in the dining area, and they included Australian Marc Leishman who was sat on his own, and three Americans who were in lively conversation at another table, and these included the 2012 US Open champion, Webb Simpson, and the 2007 Masters champion, Zach Johnson. They were all a bit put out by the fact that the tournament had run into an unscheduled fifth day, and they were wondering how they might get home, and they were offering each other a lift back home on their private jets!

Funny to think that St Andrews' first Open Champion in 1873, Tom Kidd, won just £11; In 1984 Spain's golfing matador, Seve Ballesteros, won £50,000, and big hitting John Daly £125,000 in 1995. By 2000, the prize money in golf was really taking off, and Tiger Woods would win £500,000 for winning at St Andrews that year, and just five years later, Louis Oosthuizen would bank £850,000. The 2015 winner would be crowned in about 24 hours time, and whoever that might be, he was set to take home £1,150,000, so it is little wonder that some of the modern players can afford their own plane.

Having found a Premier Inn in Dundee at great expense on Sunday night, the following morning we made our way to the Old Course for about 10 o'clock. Play had started at 7.45am, but with 40 groups playing in pairs, there was something to see all day, and thankfully the weather forecast was good for the whole day. With full access to seating anywhere around the course, I decided my best option was to sit in the stand by the first tee and immediately behind the 18th green, which would allow a perfect view of the opening tee shots, and the 1st green, and also the 17th green, as well as a full view of the spectacular 18th hole, where with a bit of luck an exciting finish would play out.

Decision made, I made my way up to the top tier of the stand, picnic left overs and juice to hand, and settled in for the day. The views were stunning, across the links land, with all those iconic buildings to my left, and St Andrews Bay in the distance, and the atmosphere, though perhaps not the throng of people that you would expect on a normal Sunday afternoon finish, built beautifully through the day as the contest played out to a thrilling climax.

Of the 14 players in the mix, Danny Willett who would go on to be the surprise 2016 winner of the US Masters teed off with Zach Johnson at 1.30pm, and the leading pair of Louis Oosthuizen and Paul Dunne got underway at 2.30pm. The early starters were finishing their rounds and scoring was proving quite difficult with only a few rounds in the 60s, including two 66s from Scott Arnold and Brendon Todd, and it is usually tougher for the last groups as they have to cope with the pressure of winning the tournament as well.

After twelve holes of the final round two shots separated five players, with Zach Johnson and Marc Leishman both bogey free and seven birdies to the good, they led on sixteen under par, a shot ahead of Oosthuizen, and two shots ahead of Day and Spieth, the latter having double bogeyed the 8th. Johnson bogeyed the 13th and 17th, but crucially, and right in front of us, holed from about 25 foot above the hole on the last green to post fifteen under par, whilst at the same time giving the crowd a huge fist pump. Leishman had command of the tournament and stood on the 16th tee with a one shot lead, but bogeyed the hole, and finished with two pars to match Johnson's round of 66, and his fifteen under par total.

Day and Spieth were playing together and both arrived on

the 18th tee having made brave par fours at the Road Hole, knowing that they needed a birdie to get into a play off. In Spieth's case, he was still walking in the footsteps of Arnold Palmer who back in 1960 had won both the Masters and US Open, and came to St Andrews for a hat-trick of major wins, and Spieth like Palmer would narrowly miss out on his birdie, as would Jason Day, both crestfallen in their final moment of disappointment. Only Louis Oosthuizen could now join the play-off, and at the last hole the South African nervelessly sent a short iron approach to six feet from the hole and calmly slotted home the birdie putt to card a three under par score of 69, and join Leishman and Johnson in a three way play-off!

Johnson had finished over an hour ago, Leishman half an hour before Oosthuizen, and the crowd sensed that Oosthuizen was now favourite to win, partly because his eye was in, and he was buoyed by a birdie at the last, but also because he had previously won at St Andrews. However, the Open play-off is now decided over four holes, so this meant that we would have another hour to wait before we knew the outcome, and over four holes lots of things can happen, especially at the Road Hole. The four play-off holes were the 1st, 2nd, 17th and 18th holes, so I was definitely in the best spot to see the action unfold, and I therefore remained glued to my seat, which I was not about to give up for anything or anyone, and it is amazing how long you can last without going to the toilet if you really need to!

Things got off to a hot start when both Oosthuizen and Johnson birdied the first, whilst Leishman bogeyed to fall two behind and in effect fall out of the race. Zach Johnson's putter had been hot all day, and he rolled in another birdie on the second hole to take a one shot lead. All three struggled on the Road Hole, and made bogeys, Oosthuizen finally showing a chink in his armour when he missed from five or six foot for par, so it was all down to the 18th, and both players played excellent approach shots above the hole, Johnson went first on a similar line to earlier, but only half the distance, and missed on the right, which gave Oosthuizen one more chance, but his 10 foot putt which was beautifully struck lipped out and the 39 year Iowan, Zach Johnson, was Open Champion.

The closing ceremony quickly followed, and there was no doubting how much this meant to Zach Johnson, who had come through a long and at times difficult week, and quoted "patience and perseverance" as the cornerstones of his victory, and finding it difficult to describe his feelings, he added that "he was honoured, humbled and thankful to win at the birth place of golf – that jug means so much in sports, and in our own sport. I can't play any better than I did. I just stayed in it, waited for the opportunities, and made a few putts". They do say golf is a simple game.

St Andrews was due to stage the 2021 Open, but because of coronavirus, and the cancellation of the 2020 championship, this has been put back a year to July 2022, when the 150th Open championship will fittingly be decided at the spiritual home of golf. Perhaps Rory McIlroy or Jordan Spieth or Brooks Koepka will triumph? Whoever wins, they will need to strive every ounce as hard as Zach Johnson did, and of course they will need to bring their A game, and deal with moments of bad luck, as well as good fortune. St Andrews is a special place to visit and the Old Course is a must to play for any golfer, and whilst I am not sure the excitement of 2015 can be replicated, I can't wait for the next chapter to be written.

Bibliography, additional sources and thanks:

Where possible, I have used my own sources which includes schoolboy diaries, holiday diaries, memoirs, retained scorecards, match day programmes, newspaper cuttings, poems and memorabilia, all of which have contributed in differing degrees and helped bring back to life the described events in this book.

Chapter 1:
YouTube: Malcolm MacDonald (SUPER MAC) His greatest goal ever? The clip is 4 minutes 46 seconds and listen out for Barry Davies' description of the wonder goal!

Chapter 2:
Fire and Ashes – How Yorkshire's finest took on the Australians. *(Great Northern Books)*
The Official History of Yorkshire County Cricket Club. *(Derek Hodgson)*
Magnificent Seven – Yorkshire's Championship Years. The Players' Own Story, with Andrew Collomosse *(Great Northern Books)*
Test Match Special and YouTube – commentary and visuals when Jonathan Agnew drew Geoff Boycott – hilarious!

Chapter 3:
Seve the Movie *(produced by Entertainment in Video)*
Thanks to Billy Foster for the stories about Seve.
The Ryder Cup – an Illustrated History by Dale Concannon *(Aurum)*
The Greatest Game Ever Played by Mark Frost – a great telling of the pioneers of golf in the modern era, interwoven around the incredible story of the 1913 US Open, and probably the best golf book ever.

Chapter 4:
The World's Greatest Cricket Matches – Norman Giller *(Octopus Books)*
Botham – Head On, the Autobiography *(Ebury Press)*
Ian Botham on Cricket *(Cassell)*
DVD Set: "English Cricket's Greatest Ever Matches" *(Sharp Focus production for Green Umbrella)*

Chapter 5:

The Official History of the Ryder Cup – Michael Williams *(Stanley Paul)*

YouTube 1977 British Open – Duel in the Sun *(11.18 minute clip)*

YouTube The Duel in the Sun – I Was There – by Andrew Proud.

Thanks to the Miller Family, Dennis Watson and Royal Birkdale Golf Club.

Chapter 6:

John Hendrie - for his personal insights and anecdotes.

Telegraph and Argus, thanks to their match day reporter, David Markham, and also to Bill Marshall.

Chapter 7:

John Helm, John Hendrie and David Markham for their personal recollections.

Paul Town for creating the special edition print "56"

The Story of the Bradford Fire: Martin Fletcher *(Bloomsbury)*

Of Boars and Bantams: *(Temple Printing)*

One Day in May: The Story of the Bradford Fire (2015) – documentary presented by Gabby Logan, produced by Tenmonkeys on Vimeo

Chapter 8:

Thanks to Sarah Gillbard (nee Hawthorne) for inviting me to Adelaide.

Adelaide Alive Poster – thanks to the Australian Grand Prix Corporation and the South Australia State Library.

Chapter 9:

Underarm Incident in 1981 Aus Vs NZ (most disgraceful moment in cricket history) – YouTube

Sport's Great All-Rounders by James Holder *(Author House)*

Chapter 10:

Thanks to Andy Locke for his recollections of the drive home, and to Tony Speight for capturing the day so brilliantly on camera.

Chapter 11:

Thanks also to my co-spectators, Paul and Oliver Gillbard and James Snook.

Chapter 12:
Thanks in particular to the Barmy Army, David Palmer, Robbie Hatfield and the BBC.

Chapter 13:
Thanks to Thomas Cook for the tickets, and to all the Games Makers and Athletes who contributed so much to make London 2012 arguably the best Olympics ever.

Chapter 14:
Thank you to my companions on the day, Alex McIntosh, Sam Ridgway and Richard Coakes.

Chapter 15:
Thanks to Andrew Jennings for this great opportunity. If ever there was an example of the benefit of spontaneity and watching live sport to the very end, surely this was one of the best and most unpredictable of outcomes.

Websites used to help with research:
cricketarchive.com
en.wikipedia.org
espncricinfo.com
f1destinations.com
opengolf.com

I Wished I Was There
Coming Soon….

As I wrote "I Was There" It quickly dawned on me that there were so many more sporting events that I wished I had been able to attend. So my idea for a second book was simply to capture the best of these, and having already made a long list, I realised that it was not going to be easy to restrict my selections to a top 15.

This is where you might be able to help me? I would welcome your own individual recollections of great sporting moments that you have either witnessed, or seen live on TV. All you need to do is send me an email before March 31st 2021 of not more than 100 words to robinsnooky@gmail.com, detailing the 4 W's (When, Where, Who and Why?), and don't forget to put your personal stamp on your story.

The book will span over 50 years, and will start with the 1966 World Cup Final which (apparently) I watched live sitting on my grandfather's knee, and will climax with Ben Stokes' extraordinary Headingley Test of 2019, which I listened to spellbound on the car radio whilst on holiday on the East Coast of Yorkshire in Ravenscar.

Robin Snook